A Bird-watche
Evening
Coot and

**Books should be returned on or before the
last date stamped below.**

**NORTH EAST of SCOTLAND LIBRARY SERVICE
MELDRUM MEG WAY, OLDMELDRUM**

A Bird-watcher's Quiz Book

Evenings at the Coot and Corncrake

COMPILED BY
Chris Harbard

CARTOONS BY
Paul Cemmick

ADDITIONAL ILLUSTRATION BY
Robert Gillmor

MISLEADING NOTEBOOK ILLUSTRATIONS BY
Crispin Fisher

COLLINS
8 Grafton Street London W1

First published by William Collins Sons & Co Ltd 1986
Planned and Produced by Robert MacDonald Publishing
© in the text Chris Harbard 1986
© in the cartoon illustrations Paul Cemmick 1986
© in additional illustration Robert Gillmor 1986
© in notebook illustrations Crispin Fisher 1986

ISBN 0 00 219834 7

Typeset by Wordsmiths Graphics Ltd, London
Printed and bound in Great Britain by William Collins Sons & Co
Ltd, Glasgow

Contents

Preface

In writing these tales from the *Coot and Corncrake*, the names of the individuals have been changed to protect their reputations. The location of the pub has also been made deliberately obscure, and should you happen to stumble across somewhere that fits the description then beware, for you might one day find yourself featuring in a future story of that celebrated establishment.

The *Coot and Corncrake* is by no means as untypical as some of you might suspect: such places do exist, and they are populated by regulars who may sometimes bear an uncanny resemblance to the characters portrayed in this book. You may well know some. If you wonder if you resemble any of them yourself, you are recommended to complete the test questions in 'So You Think You're a Twitcher' on page 110.

The quiz evenings in the *Coot and Corncrake* are one of the most popular events in the wintertime. The quizzes in this book have been drawn from them. Each quiz is composed of 64 questions, with the specific intention of allowing their use in team competitions. In this case the format is as follows. Each of the two teams is composed of four players and each quiz is divided into eight rounds with four questions to each team per round. Two rounds are treated as individual questions, with the rest being answered by the whole team together.

The quizzes can of course be used entirely informally, whether among a group, between two consenting (or even dissenting) adults or simply on your own. The latter course might in fact avoid some of the ill-temper and general unpleasantness that they have unfortunately caused, on more than one occasion, in the bar of the *Coot and Corncrake*.

Whatever the case, I hope that all who use this book will find some entertainment, and more than a little enlightenment, within its pages.

Chris Harbard. *August 1986*

To all bird-watchers everywhere, this book is
respectfully dedicated

The barred Warbler

It was a quiet evening in the *Coot and Corncrake*. The Colonel was sitting on his stool at the corner of the bar, as he had done for more years than anyone dared to remember. A couple of strangers on a birdwatching holiday sat in the corner, writing postcards home and discussing the birds they had seen that day. Other regulars occupied their more or less accustomed places, talking quietly to each other of birdwatching and other less important aspects of life.

Then a loud voice was heard outside: the door opened and two men walked in. Twitchett and Stringwell had arrived. Twitchett, the owner of the loud voice, was a large man with a rather florid complexion and an exaggerated military bearing. Stringwell, by contrast, was a much smaller, paler, thin-faced man, with a slightly furtive expression. They were both regulars as well as keen birdwatchers, and they frequently travelled around together in their search for the interesting or unusual.

As Stringwell claimed possession of their favourite seats by the window, Twitchett moved purposefully to the bar. As always, he paused for a moment to admire the dusty glass case kept permanently on a shelf above the optics. Inside the case was a piece of local history, a faded shape, barely discernible as a bird, but representing (according to the label) the only British record of a Whip-poor-will. It had been shot by Twitchett's great-grandfather in 1883, reputedly just after he had left the pub one night. You won't find it on the British list today, however, since it was removed as one of the infamous 'Halstead Rarities'. This did nothing to diminish Twitchett's satisfaction in the exhibit. Finally, turning his attention back to the barmaid, he ordered two pints of best bitter and returned to the waiting Stringwell.

At this moment, the pub door opened again and admitted a tall thin character dressed in a Barbour jacket, wellington boots and a woolly hat with a badge bearing the slogan 'Birders

Against the Bomb'. It was Tom Stickler, known to his birding friends as 'Dipstick'. He was always dressed in this fashion, and rumour had it that he wore the same garb to bed.

'You're late' said Stringwell.

'I've been looking for Dotterel' said Stickler.

'Enjoy your trip?' quipped Twitchett.

'No. I dipped out again. I don't believe they really exist, or else they must have been Dutch birds. Any decent British ones would have waited for me.'

'That's funny' exclaimed Stringwell. 'They looked settled when I saw them; they must have gone just after I left.'

Stickler grunted. This was one of Stringwell's classic phrases. He seemed to have a knack of seeing birds other people missed, or of seeing twice as many as anyone else. Stickler ordered himself a pint and joined the other two. Over in the corner, the strange couple had finished writing postcards and appeared to be trying to identify something from a field guide.

'Twitchett had a Hobby over the marsh this afternoon' announced Stringwell. 'That's his third this week.'

Stringwell winced. 'All I ever see there are Kestrels' he said. Twitchett looked pleased; he seemed to be about to say something when the phone rang. It was for Stringwell.

'News at last' said Stringwell as he walked to the bar. 'Hallo... yes... where?... when?' his voice began to rise in excitement. 'Is it still there?   OK, thanks'. He came back to the table. 'Terek Sandpiper at Minsmere' he said eagerly, 'found this afternoon. It spent the afternoon in front of the Scrape hide. Who's coming for it?'

'They're one day birds' said Stickler dismissively, 'at least they've always gone when I get there.'

'I've already seen a couple.' said Twitchett. 'Count me out.'

'But it might still be worth going' pleaded Stringwell, 'there could be lots of other migrants around.'

Twitchett, however, was in the mood for reminiscence: he had no intention of losing his audience. 'Y'know' he said firmly 'this reminds me of the day I saw my first Terek Sandpiper, must have been back in '72.' He settled into his chair and began to light a pipe.

'It was' he said between puffs 'a clear calm day with a light easterly blowing. I'd been down to the marsh in the early morning and saw a couple of Wood Sandpipers, a Blue-headed Wagtail and a Hobby. After breakfast I decided to go down to the point and see if there were any migrants. On the way there,

I notched up a couple of Redstarts, a few Wheatears and a late Fieldfare. Suddenly, from one of the bushes came a loud tacking sound which had to come from a warbler. Sure enough, as I approached the bush, a small bird flitted out and along to the next bush. I only got a brief view of the little blighter, but I had this feeling that I might be onto something. Through my binoculars, I could only see a movement within the bush until the bird hopped into a gap. It was obviously a Sylvia warbler, but I needed to get closer to see which one. I

11

crept to the side of the bush, only to see the bird fly round behind me and land at the edge of another bush, this time out in the open but with the sun behind it. I could see no obvious markings on it, but I knew by then that it was something pretty unusual. After a good half hour of following the bird I had seen enough – greyish-brown back, pale underparts, dark eye – to convince me: it was a Barred Warbler.'

He paused for a moment, exhaling a vast plume of noxious smoke and glancing at his two companions. Stringfellow and Stickler made appropriate noises of admiration.

'The rest of the morning was almost as good. Further along the point I flushed a brown female cuckoo from a small tree and, at the same time, a greeny-yellow bird flew up from the ground and away. From its size, it could only have been a female Golden Oriole. From then on, I kept seeing good birds. A Wryneck, a female White-spotted Bluethroat and a Firecrest. Not a bad score before lunch. Then, in the afternoon I heard that a Terek Sandpiper had been seen at Minsmere. So I went and saw it.' Twitchett sighed with pleasure at the recollection. 'Definitely one of my best days' birding' he said.

A silence fell. Stringfellow and Stickler appeared to be lost for words and took refuge in their pints. They were saved by a soft female voice just behind them. 'Excuse me' it said. 'We couldn't help overhearing you. You seem to know a lot about birds, and we wondered if you could help us identify something.' The voice belonged to one of the couple in the corner, who turned out, at closer range, to be a rather attractive blonde. Twitchett leant forwards with a beam on his face.

'Certainly' he said. 'What did it look like?'

'Well, there were six of them in the field opposite the pub. We saw them this afternoon. I thought they were partridges at first. They were grey with chestnut on the belly and a distinctive white stripe above the eye and across the belly. They kept running and stopping. Only we can't find them in the book.' She looked at them expectantly.

A howl of despair and rage escaped from Stickler. He had gone slightly green. He stood up abruptly, knocking over his chair, and ran to the bar. 'Double brandy, please' he said in a choking voice as his sobs echoed through the bar.

Questions: *1. Why was Twitchett's Barred Warbler not accepted by the county bird recorder? 2. What was his Golden Oriole more likely to have been? 3. What are the two other errors in his story? 4. What had the two strangers seen?*

General Knowledge

1. *What do coyotes eat on television?*

2. *How many feathers are there on a swan; 15,000, 25,000 or 35,000?*

3. *Which is the odd one out: Blue Tit, Garden Warbler, Spotted Flycatcher, Robin?*

4. *Where on a bird are the lores?*

5. *Which opera features a bird-catcher?*

6. *What is a 'devil-bird'?*

7. *What famous bird escaped from London zoo?*

8. *What is a female ruff called?*

9. *What have Yellow Wagtail, Carrion Crow and Pied Wagtail in common?*

10. *Why is a Stone Curlew so named?*

11. *What bird has tippets?*

12. *What is a female swan called?*

13. *How many blackbirds were baked in a pie?*

14. *What is the collective name for penguins?*

15. *What bird doesn't give a hoot in Ireland and why?*

16. *What game bird sounds thirsty?*

17. *What is the American equivalent of the R.S.P.B.?*

18. *What bird is collectively known as a charm?*

19. Which is the odd one out: Marsh, Wood, Willow, Garden?

20. What is the most numerous British breeding bird?

21. Where is England's only gannetry?

22. What is a female Black Grouse called?

23. What is Britain's smallest bird of prey?

24. Which is the odd one out: Willow Warbler, Dartford Warbler, Reed Warbler, Grasshopper Warbler?

25. Where do Manx Shearwaters spend the winter?

26. What bird sings 'a little bit of bread and no cheese'?

27. What is the collective name for Swans?

28. What birds are known as loons in North America?

29. What bird was used 'instead of a cross'?

30. What does the British Trust for Ornithology have for its emblem?

31. What is South America's equivalent of the Emu?

32. What British naturalist has a thrush named after him?

33. Which is the odd one out: Tern, Gull, Skua, Sandpiper?

34. What are Sawbills?

35. What famous bird breeds at Loch Garten?

36. What bird is collectively known as a 'murmuration'?

37. The convict Robert Stroud wrote a book about bird diseases. Where?

38. What island is a Gannet specifically named after?

39. What common British bird was first seen there in 1952?

40. Which is the odd one out: Dunlin, Turnstone, Purple Sandpiper, Redshank?

41. What bird was 'Martha' who died in Cincinnati Zoo in 1914?

42. What is a 'titlark'

43. What birds are kept in the Tower of London?

44. How do you distinguish between male and female Great Spotted Woodpeckers?

45. Which birds were invaluable to coal miners?

46. Which now widespread British bird was confined to St Kilda until 1878?

47. What colour are wild Budgerigars?

48. What bird sounds 'frank'?

49. Where was Britain's first bird observatory?

50. What are boobies?

51. What finch is called a 'Grosbec' in France?

52. What is a bonxie?

53. What is the collective name for Snipe?

54. Which species of owl is most cosmopolitan?

55. Which British breeding bird has a recurved bill?

56. Which bird helped Oscar Wilde's Happy Prince to relieve the poor?

57. Which bird sleeps on the wing?

58. Which bird had a pussycat for a friend?

59. Which is the odd one out: Marsh, Great, Willow, Bearded?

60. What was the bird trained by T.H. White?

61. What is a raptor?

62. How do you tell the difference between the British and continental races of the Dipper?

63. What is a windhover?

64. Which moping bird 'did to the moon complain' and in which famous poem?

It is New Year's Day, and Twitchett is doing a Sponsored Bird-Watch in aid of the British Trust for Ornithology; so he's writing down all the bird species he sees. Here are two pages of the day's notes.

0900 Drive GRENDON → WILLEN   1st Jan. 19:4

Collared Dove
Carrion Crow   Stock Dove
Rook
Starling
Pheasant
Magpie   Black-headed Gull
Swallow   with Lapwings
Skylark   Blackbird
Dunnock   Jackdaw
Green Woodpecker   House Sparrow

0945 WILLEN BALANCING LAKE

Goldeneye   Mute Swan
   3 ♂'s   Mallard
                                      Grey Heron
                                      Canada Goose
Shoveler   3 Greylag
   all ♂'s c. 25

                                                      glide
Tufted Duck
Pochard   Barn Owl
Teal   quartering island
Coot

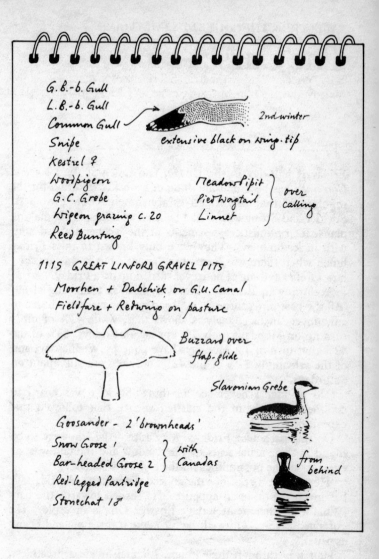

G.B.-b. Gull
L.B.-b. Gull
Common Gull
Snipe
Kestrel ♀
Woodpigeon
G.C. Grebe
Wigeon grazing c. 20
Reed Bunting

2nd winter
extensive black on wing-tip

Meadow Pipit ⎫
Pied Wagtail ⎬ over calling
Linnet ⎭

1115 GREAT LINFORD GRAVEL PITS

Moorhen + Dabchick on G.U. Canal
Fieldfare + Redwing on pasture

Buzzard over
flap-glide

Slavonian Grebe

Goosander - 2 'brownheads'
Snow Goose 1
Bar-headed Goose 2 ⎫ with
                    ⎬ Canadas
Red-legged Partridge
Stonechat 1♂

from behind

Questions: *1. Which bird was it really impossible for Twitchett to have seen? 2. If Twitchett's Bird-Watch had been competitive, which further two species would have been disallowed? 3. Which two birds did he misidentify, and what were they really?*

17

The Curse

Friday is half-day in the village, and lunch at the *Coot and Corncrake* has become something of a weekly tradition for the regulars of that celebrated establishment. For Twitchett, Stickler and Stringwell, it had become an occasion for making plans, for optimistic assessments of the weekend ahead and, with luck, for news. They were only known to miss Friday lunch when there was 'something about', but it was amazing how rarely anything of note ever turned up on a Friday.

According to Listman, however, it wasn't amazing at all. 'All the best birds turn up on Mondays', he was once heard to announce. 'In fact, analysis shows that, while 42% of birds turn up on Mondays, only 7% appear on Fridays: 63% of the 42% that turn up on Mondays have gone by Wednesday, and of the remaining 37% of the 42%, only 6% are still about on Saturdays.'

'No wonder I never see anything' Stickler was heard to comment bitterly in the startled silence that followed this exposition.

On this particular Friday – May 13th – the trio were to be found in their usual seats by the window and the talk was, as ever, about the possibilities for the coming weekend.

'How about a spot of lunch?' said Twitchett. 'All this talk has given me quite an appetite.' He turned towards the bar. 'What's on the menu today, Rossie? Quails in aspic?' He guffawed loudly. 'Oh well, better make it three pie and beans as usual.'

Half way through their lunch, Listman made a breathless entrance. 'Golden Oriole' he announced. 'In the little copse – a cracking male.' Stringwell and Stickler were on their feet immediately. But Twitchett didn't move a muscle. Indeed, within a few seconds he had gone a disturbing grey colour, and little beads of perspiration were beginning to form on his forehead. His eyes were staring and he appeared to have gone into a trance. He was mumbling incoherently. Stringwell and

Stickler stared at him anxiously. The only words they could make out sounded like 'cold and wet.'

'He's raving' decided Stickler, 'it's a lovely day outside.'

Twitchett started to come round. 'You all right Twitchett?' asked Stringwell.

'Yes, yes I'm OK' lied Twitchett. 'You chaps carry on. Must have been a bad pie or something.'

'There's nothing wrong with my pies' exclaimed Rossi indignantly.

'There's nothing wrong with mine either' barked the Colonel as he attempted to carve his way through the plastic wrapping on his Cornish pastie. 'Old nose is not so good these days though. No aroma to this pie at all.'

'We'll probably see you down there a bit later then' said Stringwell as he and Stickler made hurriedly for the door. But they didn't, and it was much later that day before they saw Twitchett again.

By half-past eight, the *Coot and Corncrake* was beginning to fill up, and Twitchett was already ensconced in his favourite chair by the time the others returned. His colour was back to normal and, with a pint of best bitter and a whisky in front of him, it was obvious that his stomach had not suffered any lasting effects from his lunchtime experiences.

'Made me feel like Crippen' complained Rossie to Mr Burke, the pale-faced local undertaker, whose preference for vodka and tomato juice was considered by many to be singularly unfortunate. In the window seat, Twitchett's court had once again convened and Stringwell and Stickler were enthusing about the afternoon's bird. 'Brilliant' said Stringwell.

'Ace' echoed Stickler.

'Pity you had that funny turn' said Stringwell, turning to Twitchett. 'Are you OK now? It's not like you to miss a bird like that.'

'Fine thanks. Actually chaps, it wasn't quite what it seemed, so you don't have to worry about eating Rossie's pies in future. It was …' He paused, as if reluctant to continue. '…well I may as well tell you. It was 'The Curse' that did it to me.'

'The Curse!?' Stringwell exclaimed incredulously, in a voice loud enough to halt all other conversation in the bar.

'That's right', said Twitchett settling back into his chair and removing his pipe from his pocket. 'The Curse of the Twitchetts. Let me tell you the story.'

'It all started over 70 years ago in the United States, where you'll remember my great-great uncle Eustace had emigrated.

Like his brother, my great-great grandfather Peregrine, Eustace was an inveterate traveller, and it was in the summer of 1911 that his wanderings took him on that fateful journey to Arizona. It was still a time of change and unrest in that part of the world. The Mexican civil war had just ended; Arizona was about to become a US state and, although it was 25 years after Geronimo's final surrender at Skeleton Canyon, there were still occasional problems with hostile Indians.'

'Bouncers' barked the Colonel. 'Hall and Griffiths were the worst – always very hostile.'

'They were West Indian bowlers' corrected Rossie unwisely as a ripple of laughter went round the bar.

'Nonsense. The best Indian bowlers were the spinners' announced the Colonel, with such a defiant shake of his head that the earpiece of his hearing aid flew out of his ear and did a quick leg-break into Mr Burke's Bloody Mary, where it became irreparably clogged up with congealing tomato juice.

Twitchett boomed on regardless. 'According to Eustace's diary he travelled south from Tucson to Douglas on the Mexican border, from where he planned to explore the spectacular Chiricahua Mountains, once the home of the Apache chief Cochise and now regarded as one of the best birding spots in America. He particularly wanted to see as many as he could of the dozen or so humming birds of the area, but his major quest was to discover the first nest of that Mexican speciality, the Coppery-tailed Trogon. For nearly a fortnight he scoured the canyons in vain. There were birds everywhere – Montezuma Quails, Black Phoebes, Brown Towhees and Blue-grey Gnatcatchers – a seemingly endless catalogue of exotic names. But no Trogons. There were, however, humming birds galore; Black-chinned and Broad-tailed; Ruby-throated and Broad-billed; Violet-crowned and Rivoli's.'

'But time was beginning to run out for Eustace. Both he and his supplies were almost exhausted and he was on the verge of abandoning his quest when, on Friday 13th July, he found it.' Here Twitchett paused, with considerable dramatic effect, and began to refill his pipe.

'Found what?' exclaimed Stickler impatiently, 'the nest?'.

Twitchett was enjoying himself. Slowly he lit his briar. 'The 'hidden canyon' 'he said, in an exaggerated whisper. An expectant hush fell over the bar. Twitchett was once again where he liked to be most; at the centre of attention. 'Eustace had come across a narrow, steep-sided canyon which was particularly interesting for the number of caves that were evident in the rocky sides. A bird of prey suddenly came into view. It was a medium-sized, pale sandy-brown falcon with creamy streaked underparts and its fast manoeuverable flight took it up to a rocky ledge some 100ft above the canyon floor. He decided to climb up to the ledge and some 10 minutes later he was close to the spot where the bird had disappeared. Of the bird there was no sign, but Eustace soon realised that he was standing close to the narrow entrance of a deep cave. Always the intrepid explorer – as are all Twitchetts – he began to investigate and soon found that the narrow entrance disguised what gradually turned out to be a cave of huge proportions. Suddenly, the silence was broken by a thunderous flapping noise as a cloud of bats – 'thousands' according to Eustace's diary – erupted from the roof of the cave.'

'Vampires' hissed Listman mockingly and Mr Burke ordered another drink. Twitchett scowled.

'Startled, he turned to run but lost his footing and suddenly he was falling down a steep gulley in the cave wall. It was all over in a matter of seconds.'

'Unlike Twitchett's stories' whispered Stringwell to Stickler, and was promptly quelled by a glare from Twitchett.

'As I was saying' he growled, 'Eustace found himself looking at a stream of light that was coming from what appeared to be another entrance to the cave. Uninjured and relieved, he dusted himself down and walked purposefully towards the light. As he came out into the open, he could hardly believe his eyes, for it was not the canyon that he had been in only 10 minutes previously. Instead, he found himself gazing down into a steep-sided, bowl-shaped crater which seemed to blaze with colour from every quarter. The rose-coloured cliffs were speckled with bright green lichen and the valley floor was dotted with copses of white-trunked sycamores, black walnuts and Apache pines. And everywhere there were birds. More birds than he had ever seen before. There were hummingbirds and kingbirds to be seen with every glance. Sulphur-bellied Flycatchers and Painted Redstarts appeared to be in every tree. And, above all, there were trogons. It seemed to Eustace that almost every sycamore had one. From his distant viewpoint, he could see that the ground below the sycamores was mottled with little patches of white. 'Trogon eggs at last' he exclaimed.

As he marvelled at the elegant beauty of the birds in their striking plumage of reds and greens, his thoughts drifted to the accolades that would soon be bestowed on him. Eustace Twitchett, the man who found the trogons' nests! Twitchett

Canyon, pehaps? It was surely the pinnacle of his career. A clutch of eggs was what he needed now and he began to make his descent to the bottom of the canyon.

As he did so, he began to fell distinctly uneasy, for there was something rather eerie about this beautiful place hidden away from the rest of the world. "Eustace Twitchett go home" a voice seemed to whisper in his mind's ear. By the time he had reached the sycamores, the unease had developed into positive fear – a sensation virtually unknown to Twitchetts.' Twitchett pushed out his chest and settled deeper into his chair, the lunchtime incident seemingly fogotten. 'Anyway,' he continued, 'there was Eustace desperately fighting his urge to turn and run, but still driven by his determination to leave with a clutch of trogon's eggs. And that was when he saw the bones!'

A gasp came from the audience and at this point even Mr Burke began to take an interest in the story. 'There were bones everywhere. Big bones and little bones: arms, legs and even skulls. The whole clearing was white with them, and right in the middle was a totem pole and on the top of the pole was a bird ...' Twitchett paused '...a Scotts Oriole' he finished with a flourish. 'By now, Eustace was almost paralysed with fear. He stood motionless, his right hand tightly clenching the small revolver in his pocket. When the wizened figure of the ancient Indian appeared, he was so scared he almost shot himself! The Indian was old. Very old. His skin had the look of weather-beaten leather and his stooping gait gave him a hunched appearance. In his hand, he carried a forked stick, and in his headband was a solitary black and yellow feather.'

' "Accursed paleface" he screamed at Eustace. "You dare defile the happy hunting ground of my forefathers. A curse upon you and your family." He removed the feather from his headband and waved it accusingly at Eustace and then began dance in circles around him, leaping and weaving and crouching, until Eustace was completely mesmerised. And all the time, in a high pitched wailing voice, he chanted continually "Misfortune e'er will you beset if you behold the gold and jet – a curse on those whom you beget." '

'In his diary Eustace never really explained how he managed to get out of the canyon' continued Twitchett. 'All he could remember was that he ran. Ran faster than he had ever run before – trogons' eggs were the last things on his mind at that point.

Although he later drew a detailed map of his route, nobody then or since has ever managed to find the 'hidden canyon' of

the trogons, and it wasn't until much later that the first trogon's nest in Arizona was eventually found.'

'In 1939 actually' chipped in Listman, but Twitchett paid him no attention.

'As for poor old Eustace, well, as most of you know the end came just a few months later north of Los Angeles when he was attacked – on Friday 13th April 1912 – by a tiger that had escaped from a travelling circus in Santa Barbara. He was on his way to Los Padres for the 'big one' when it happened, but it wasn't to be. The Curse of the Twitchetts saw to that!'

'What a load of old cobblers' pronounced Listman in the silence that followed Twitchett's narrative. 'Statistically highly improbable, but mere coincidence nevertheless.'

'Coincidence is it?' said Twitchett, plainly nettled. 'Then perhaps you can tell us the statistical likelihood of my grandfather Bartholomew Twitchett being knocked down by a tram – a black and yellow tram, mark you – on Friday 13th June 1931 in Gateshead High Street. Or of young Billy Twitchett, my nephew, slipping on a rotten banana skin and cracking his skull open in Kings Lynn when going for the Great White Egret on Friday May 13th 1979. And only a couple of years ago I had a very nasty incident myself with some Hull City supporters whilst waiting for a train in Potters Bar. Friday January 13th 1984 that was. So now you can see why there was no way I could take a chance today.'

'Well' said Stringwell, getting to his feet 'it was a grand yarn. One of your best. Now, how about a drink?'

'Give him an Advocaat with a black olive' suggested Listman unkindly.

Twitchett ignored him. 'Thanks, I'll have a .. AAAAARGH!' With a blood-curdling scream that stopped the entire pub in its tracks, Twitchett suddenly rocketed to his feet and careered wildly towards the gents, with a look of naked terror on his already ashen face. 'I'm done for. It's the Curse.'

In the shocked silence that followed his disappearance, a low buzzing drew everybody's attention. There, on the seat of Twitchett's chair, was a large black and yellow hornet.

Questions: *1. Which bird did Eustace wrongly claim to have seen in Arizona? 2. What was the 'big one' he was going to see? 3. What was the bird of prey Eustace saw? 4. What is the Coppery-tailed Trogon now called and what did Eustace clearly not know about it?*

Bird Behaviour

1. *How does a Nuthatch adjust the size of its nest hole?*

2. *How are seabirds adapted to drinking salt water?*

3. *What is anting?*

4. *What is allopreening?*

5. *What British birds pass food to each other in flight as part of their courtship?*

6. *Why would a Ringed Plover appear to have a broken wing?*

7. *What is whiffling?*

8. *What does crepuscular mean when applied to a bird?*

9. *How do sparrows drink?*

10. *How do pigeons drink?*

11. *What is a Mute Swan doing if it is busking?*

12. *What British bird churrs?*

13. *What is a pelagic bird?*

14. *What is an irruption?*

15. *Which birds have asymmetric ears?*

16. *Which British breeding bird has the specific name* parasiticus *and why?*

17. *How do Swallows drink?*

18. *How do sandgrouse take water to their young?*

19. Which bird spits oil when annoyed?

20. Which bird has been known to hibernate?

21. What do cave swifts and the cave-dwelling Oilbird have that other birds don't?

22. What birds thought that Konrad Lorenz was their mother?

23. What is a granivorous bird?

24. What is a graminivorous bird?

25. What is a nidifugous species?

26. What is a nidicolous species?

27. Which British bird mates in flight?

28. Which British wader 'drums'?

29. Which British passerine produces a pellet made mainly of corn husks?

30. Which British bird produces a pellet of wax?

31. Which British duck whistles?

32. Which British passerine feeds under water?

33. What is the display flight of the Woodcock called?

34. Which British bird makes a sound called 'rookooing'?

35. Why do many gulls have a red spot on their yellow bill?

36. Which bird is well known for cracking open eggs with a stone?

37. Which British bird uses an anvil?

38. What is a bower birds 'bower'?

39. What is special about the Woodpecker Finch's method of feeding?

40. What are the three commonest host birds of the Cuckoo in Britain?

41. What is a frugivorous bird?

42. Which birds use filtration feeding?

43. What is mobbing?

44. Why do gulls foot-paddle?

45. What is a piscivorous bird?

46. What is brood parasitism?

47. Which birds impale their food on thorns?

48. What is 'stooping'?

49. How does a young cuckoo ensure that it gets enough food?

50. What was a tit first observed doing in Southampton in 1921?

51. Which birds 'spin' on the water to feed?

52. Why does the Eleonora's Falcon breed in the autumn?

53. Which British bird of prey feeds on Swallows and martins?

54. How do Gannets incubate their eggs?

55. Which birds 'toboggan' as a means of locomotion?

56. Which birds are named after their domed mud nests built on branches?

57. Why are oxpeckers so called?

58. What is a 'dread' of gulls or terns?

59. Why is ecdysis so important to a bird's feathers?

60. Why are Mute Swans prone to lead poisoning?

61. What is a Black Grouse 'lek'?

62. What do tits do that has been copied by House Sparrows, Greenfinches and Siskins?

63. How can you tell feral from wild Greylag Geese, apart from by their distribution?

64. How does a phalarope's breeding differ from that of most other waders?

Rumours of a suppressed rarity in Sussex tempted Twitchett to spend a day there. Here are two of his notebook pages.

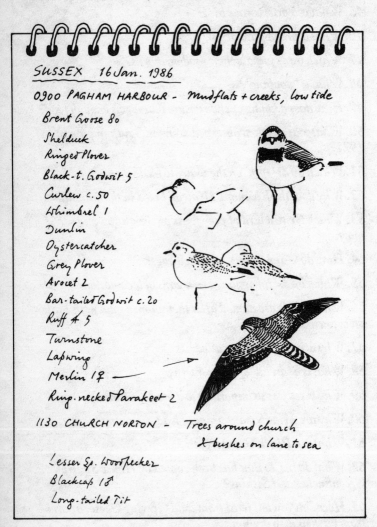

SUSSEX 16 Jan. 1986

0900 PAGHAM HARBOUR - mudflats + creeks, low tide

Brent Goose 80
Shelduck
Ringed Plover
Black-t. Godwit 5
Curlew c. 50
Whimbrel 1
Dunlin
Oystercatcher
Grey Plover
Avocet 2
Bar-tailed Godwit c. 20
Ruff ♂ 5
Turnstone
Lapwing
Merlin 1♀ —
Ring-necked Parakeet 2

1130 CHURCH NORTON - Trees around church
                                      & bushes on lane to sea

    Lesser Sp. Woodpecker
    Blackcap 1♂
    Long-tailed Tit

Firecrest 1♂
Goldcrest 1♀?
Short-eared owl flushed from bushes
Chaffinch
Brambling } flock on plough

1400 SELSEY BILL Beach & sea-watching
Red-throated Diver 1
Black-necked Grebe 1

Herring Gull
G. B.-b. Gull
Common Gull
B.-h. Gull

Sanderling
♀ Redstart

1530 CHICHESTER GRAVEL-PITS

Great Crested Grebe
Dabchick
~~Sro~~
Smew 1♀

Tufted Duck
Pochard
Coot
Canada Goose

Questions: *1. Which bird is he unlikely to have seen? 2. Which four birds did he misidentify?*

The Duel

The *Coot and Corncrake* was full, fuller even than the night of the Christmas party. Faces that hadn't been seen for years were present and everyone was waiting for the climax to a very special event. Furthermore, it was an event whose origins lay deep in the past, at a time when the Twitchett and Gripsall families were still friends.

Twitchett's great-grandfather Peregrine and old Ingram Gripsall were both interested in birds and an amicable rivalry existed between them. Peregrine's brother Eustace had emigrated to America in search of gold. He never found it and spent most of his time travelling. Peregrine frequently visited him armed with a copy of Audubon's The Birds of America. It was on one of these visits that he learned how to shoot, taught by Buffalo Bill it was said. Certainly after that visit he became one of the foremost and infamous collector of birds in Britain and it was this collecting that caused the rift between the two families.

Peregrine Twitchett had a comprehensive collection of birds that he had shot including some quite unusual ones. However after his trips to America he regularly began to find new species for Britain, all of which were American. One of these, the famous Whip-poor-will could be seen above the bar in the *Coot and Corncrake*.

Ingram Gripsall was at first enthusiastic about Peregrine's achievements but then rapidly began to question them. He kept a strict diary and in this noted down all of Peregrine's movements and captures. He associated with Peregrine less and less and began to watch him rather than birds. On his death bed his last words were 'Never trust a Twitchett unless he's in your sights.'

The diary was left to his son and it was he who first started publicly disputing the claims of Peregrine, using the contents of the diary as evidence. Peregrine himself was old by now and did not live to see the outcome of the dispute. Well, the

outcome is now history. All of Peregrine's records of new American species were removed from the official British list and became known as the 'Halstead Rarities'. Eastern King-bird, Violet-green Swallow and Ruby-throated Hummingbird were all taken off. The hummingbird it must be said was admitted under tenuous circumstances. It had been feeding on a fuschia outside the cricket pavilion, according to Peregrine, who, not having his gun with him, collected it with a fast leg-break which not only broke the unfortunate bird's legs but caused it to disintegrate, leaving only a few scattered feathers for identification.

The accusations which were levelled at the Twitchett family as a result of Gripsall's apparant treachery caused a permanent rift between their two families and it was because of this rift that the evening's special event was taking place.

This event was the latest manifestation of the feud between the families, which had flared up again a few weeks before. Twitchett had seen a Red-footed Falcon flying over the marsh and had excitedly come to the pub to report it. Dutifully he wrote out the sighting on the blackboard outside the pub and

31

settled for a lunchtime drink. Stringwell, Stickler and others heard of his sighting and came to ask him about it.

'Was it male or female?' asked Stringwell.

'Definitely a female' replied Twitchett, 'it flew across in front of me, hovered for a few minutes and then flew off. It was basically brown but I saw its red legs clearly.'

'You'd better put that on the board so that people know what to look out for.' said Stringwell.

Twitchett walked outside and to his horror found that a line had been drawn through his sighting and the word 'string' written in after it. Now this was an accusation that Twitchett could not take lying down, nor standing up for that matter. His face began to turn a livid red and a sort of choking, spluttering sound came from his lips. He marched back into the pub.

'That damn Gripsall's been at it again ' he roared, 'this is the last straw. I'm going to sort him out once and for all.'

With that he charged out of the pub and down the road, followed a few moments later by Stringwell, Stickler and most of the lounge bar. There were only two pubs in the village and it was to the other pub, *The Black Falcon*, that Twitchett hurried. He found Gripsall sitting outside.

Algernon Gripsall was a short, thick-set man with a swarthy complexion. He had black hair, bushy eyebrows and a large bristling moustache. Beside him sat Alex ('Sandy') Piper.

'You've got a cheek' thundered Twitchett.

'I've got two actually' said Gripsall calmly, 'four if... '

'Your backside could do with a good thrashing' said Twitchett, and with that he picked up a nearby copy of British Birds, but instead of a rear attack Twitchett struck him across the cheek with it and threw it on the ground.

'My honour has been questioned and must now be satisfied' said Twitchett as Gripsall picked up the British Birds.

The 'weapons' were to be binoculars, the time a few weeks later and the place could be anywhere in the area. The winner of the duel would be the person who saw or heard the most species in 24 hours. It was agreed that seconds should be appointed; Twitchett's second would accompany Gripsall and vice-versa.

So on a warm May evening the *Coot and Corncrake*, designated as the finish, was crowded with people eagerly awaiting the outcome. The duel was due to finish at midnight and an extension until that time had been arranged by Rossie. Just after last orders the sound of a car pulling up outside the pub was heard. The door swung open and in walked Twitchett. By

32

his side was Gripsall's second, 'Sandy Piper.' Twitchett was smiling.

'What a day' he said, picking up his pint and downing it like a man who has just come off antibiotics. 'A total of 126 species, old Gripsall will never beat that. I thought I might have got more as I'd had over a ton before lunch.'

'Remember when Bradman did the same at Lords' grated the Colonel.

'Best bird of the day was a Purple Heron, down by the marsh, and it was ages before I had a Great Tit.'

'Bradman had lots of great hits' continued the Colonel.

'Plenty of waders on the marsh, I even managed to see seven different plovers. Commonest thing I missed was Tawny Owl, not in its usual spot.'

At that moment Gripsall and Stringwell walked in.

'Tough luck Gripsall' said Twitchett confidently, 'you never had a chance.'

'Don't speak too soon' said Stringwell.

'All right, how many did you get?' said Twitchett now looking mildly concerned.

'Hundred and twenty six' said Gripsall.

'My God, a draw' said Twitchett, 'we'll have to do it again. Did you miss Tawny Owl as well?'

'No, I saw it at the usual spot, but it flew off immediately, I must have scared it.' smirked Gripsall.

'There might just be time... ' said Twitchett. But at that moment the clock began to strike the hour.

Between the chimes a sound could be heard outside the pub. It was the unmistakeable hoot of a Tawny Owl.

Twitchett jumped up with glee.

'Hundred and twenty seven' he chortled, 'I heard it before the clock had finished striking.' He turned to 'Sandy' Piper who had to agree.

Black fury was on Gripsall's face. He strormed out of the pub amidst cheers and catcalls. Amongst all the back-patting and congratulations not even Twitchett noticed Rossie sneaking back into the pub with his portable tape-recorder and ringing for time.

Questions: *1. Which of Peregrine Twitchett's new species is the least likely to occur in Britain? 2. Why might Gripsall's comment on the blackboard have been right? 3. What were the seven plovers Twitchett saw?*

General Knowledge Worldwide

1. Place the following in order of size: Cassowary, Emu, Ostrich, Rhea.

2. What is the difference between the White Storks on either side of the River Elbe in Germany?

3. Which African birds are capable of digesting beeswax?

4. Which bird is collectively referred to as an exaltaion?

5. What are called chickadees in America?

6. What do the initials I.C.B.P. stand for?

7. What is Finland's commonest breeding bird?

8. What legend did the Elephant Birds of Madagascar give rise to?

9. In what countries would you find birds of paradise?

10. Where did the last Dodo die?

11. What colourful birds belong to the same order as swifts?

12. What is guano?

13. Who wrote King Solomon's Ring?

14. What is a flyway?

15. What type of bird is a sapsucker?

16. What is a tattler?

17. What birds are called sapphires, emeralds and topazes?

18. Where can you see wild Canaries?

19. How many species breed in both Britain and Japan, to the nearest 10?

20. Who won the Emu War of 1932?

21. Where would you see a Kauai O-o?

22. Where would you see a Currawong?

23. What do American call jaegers?

24. What is the American equivalent of ringing?

25. In which continent would you find a Cock-of-the-Rock?

26. What type of bird was the extinct Solitaire?

27. What bird of prey has double-jointed legs?

28. What bird is the emblem of Guatemala?

29. What bird is the emblem of France?

30. What bird is the emblem of the U.S.A.?

31. What bird is the state emblem of Western Australia?

32. What is bird's nest soup made from?

33. What is an Archaeopteryx?

34. What are ratites?

35. What type of bird is a Hammerhead?

36. What is the other name for the Whale-headed Stork of Sudan?

37. How many bird species are there in the world; 7,000, 8,000 or 9,000?

38. On what islands can you find Darwin's finches?

39. What is the largest family of non-passerines?

40. How many birds are there estimated to be in the world; 10,000 million, 100,000 million or a million million?

41. Who was the first bird 'ringer' in America?

42. Why is the Secretary Bird so called?

43. Which bird spends its entire life on water?

44. What type of bird is a noddy?

45. What type of bird is a mutton-bird?

46. What does it mean if two species are sympatric?

47. What does semipalmated mean?

48. When did the Dodo become extinct; 1562, 1662 or 1762?

49. Where do Mandarin Ducks originate?

50. Where do Ruddy Ducks originate?

51. How did the poet Aeschylus die?

52. What bird was responsible for the popping of the weasel?

53. Which bird breeds only in Spain, China and Japan?

54. Which bird breeds only in Spain and Morocco?

55. Where in the world can you find the most introduced species?

56. What bird has been introduced to the most countries?

57. What birds belong to the family Cuculidae?

58. What birds belong to the family Phasianidae?

59. Which bird has only two toes?

60. Which birds have all four toes pointing forwards?

61. Which birds' eggs are incubated in mounds of rotting vegetation?

62. Which birds commonly feed from the backs of other birds?

63. What do the Labrador Duck and the Carolina Parakeet have in common?

64. Why is a lyrebird so called?

The Visitor

Once a year, *The Coot and Corncrake* plays host to an even more motley collection of birdwatchers than usual; this is on the occasion of Twitchett's annual reunion of birdwatching companions from his recent and distant past. There are not so many now as there used to be – the hazards of life and of birwatching have taken their toll. Some have got married and seem to have lost interest (although there others who have also got married and are even more enthusiastic than they were before); poor Featherstone fell off a cliff on Rockall; X (who

37

shall be nameless) is languishing in an Eastern bloc gaol for his photographic pursuit of a rarity perched on a sensitive military installation and Y (likewise) is still serving his penance to society for showing too much interest in the avifauna of a secluded nudist colony on the Norfolk coast. Nevertheless, there are still enough birdwatchers left to make it a merry evening, and one to which the regulars of *The Coot and Corncrake* look forward with pleasurable anticipation.

One of the most faithful of the participants in this annual get-together is Ackroyd, who always like to make something of a splash on these occasions. This year, true to form, he had announced that he would be accompanied by a surprise visitor. Speculation as to the identity of this unidentified birdwatcher was intense, and, as we all gathered in the saloon bar on the appointed evening, there was a definite atmosphere of excited curiosity.

Ackroyd knows how to make an entrance. Suddenly, the door was thrown open with a bang and there he was, gesturing with a grand flourish towards the shadowy figure behind him.

'You'll never guess who I've brought along' he said, beaming triumphantly at the assembled company. And indeed he was right. The tall, fair-haired and heavily tanned individual who appeared in the doorway produced no murmur of recognition. Brows furrowed all around the bar as various birdwatchers delved unproductively into their memories. The stranger, however, didn't hesitate. He walked straight over to Twitchett, hand extended and, in a broad Australian accent said 'Hi there, Hippo'.

For once in his life, Twitchett seemed lost for words. He swallowed once or twice, and blinked rapidly, as he shook the proffered hand. Before him, we soon learned, was Phil Davis who had emigrated to Australia 20 years ago and whom he had not seen since. 'Hallo Phyllosc' he said with the suspicion of a stutter.

Twitchett, Ackroyd and Davies, Twitchett explained later, had once formed a regular birding trio. Each had been given a nickname derived from the scientific name for a warbler. Davis' christian names were Philip Oscar, which had earned him the name 'Phyllosc'. Ackroyd was 'Acro', aand Twitchett, being by some way the largest of the three, was called 'Hippo'.

'Well me old cobber' said Davis, 'How's tricks – or should I say ticks?' and he laughed uproariously in a manner he must have learned from a Kookaburra and thumped Twitchett on the back. 'Glad I could make it. I've always meant to: Ackroyd told me the date and I realised it coincided with a conference in London. So here I am.'

'Good to see you Phil' said Twitchett, with a brave attempt at bonhomie. 'I often wondered if you would make it back over here. I kept meaning to write, but... ' He tailed off, realising that Phil wasn't listening.

'Struth' said Phil, pointing, 'you've still got that moth-eaten old bird behind the bar – no not you dear.' The barmaid scowled at him as he laughed. 'And the old Colonel's stool is still there, don't tell me the old galah's still going.'

'Have a drink' offered Twitchett. 'I'm afraid there are no ice-cold tubes here.'

'Never touch them' said Phil 'can't stand that Aussie lager, even after 20 years down under. Give me a pint of best.'

Gradually, the conversation settled down and the real purpose of the evening became apparent. Reminiscences, some real and some imagined, tales of birds seen and birds missed, and of ones that got away, began to be exchanged. Unusually, Twitchett remained remarkably subdued, moodily fiddling with his moustache. His attempt to hijack the conversation, when it finally came, was half-hearted at best.

'That reminds me' he said, à propos of nothing in particular 'of a day on the south coast back in... ' But it was a feeble effort. Phil had no trouble in cutting in.

'My God Hippo' he said. 'I bet I know one story nobody's heard, a real corker. You remember the day we went down to the... no, let the rest of you guess where we were.'

'It was in September '67' he explained to the company at large. 'Twitchett and I had planned a weekend away bird-watching on our motorbikes. Steve was ill otherwise he would have been with us.' Anyone watching Twitchett would have noticed a distinct change in his appearance at these words. He went very pale and seemed to retreat into his chair, and his hands, as he fumbled with his pipe and tobacco, were visibly shaking.

'We arrived late in the evening' began Phil. 'I seem to remember that we spent the night in a bus shelter. At sun-up, we made our way to the sea-watching point. It was the best time of the year and we were expecting some pretty fabulous birdwatching. We could see gannets in the distance, most passing by but a few feeding, and we soon spotted our first shearwaters planing over the waves. The rising sun highlighted their white underparts, so they had to be Manx. Some distant skuas were harrassing passing Sandwich terns – Arctic we reckoned. After about an hour of this, Twitchett suddenly punched me in the arm and yelled "Large shearwater, flying right at about 10 o'clock, three quarters of the way out." I soon picked out a distant bird flying over the water and shearing.'

' "It's pretty pale" I said.'

' "Must be a Cory's" Hippo told me confidently. "look at the size of it." '

'By this time, he was lying on his back and had his long brass telecope out, balanced on his knee. "Can't seem to find it now" he said.'

'Well, I could see it perfectly well. "I've got it" I told him. "It's moving fast right, above the horizon. Looks like a Fulmar to me." '

' "No, I've got the Fulmar, that's not it" said Twitchett. "It must have landed on the sea." '

Phil paused and looked knowingly at his audience. Smiles broke out around the table. Twitchett, however, was looking increasingly uncomfortable. He was no longer pale, but had gone an even brighter shade of red than usual, as though he had been left out in the sun too long. 'It was a Cory's' he muttered defiantly, but nobody was listening.

'The sea passage was slow to begin with' continued Phil 'but about mid-morning the wind began to rise, and soon a good nor'-westerly was blowing. Birds were coming by thick and fast. A few Sooty Shearwaters, both Arctic and Great Skuas and a couple of Storm Petrels went past, as well as a whole load of Gannets, Kittiwakes and Fulmars.'

'Then, suddenly, I got another clout in the arm. "Petrel flying low and right, quite fast, it must be a Leach's." '

'I soon found the bird that Twitchett had seen. It was pretty small and kept disappearing behind the waves. It came closer and closer as I watched it and eventually flew right over our heads and disappeared inland.'

' "Wrong again, Twitchett" I said.'

' "Nonsense" he replied. "That wasn't it. The bird I saw flew out to sea." '

At this point, Twitchett rose noisily to his feet. Bits of his face had gone pale again, so that he looked like a well-marked Mistle Thrush's egg. 'Must pop to the little boy's room' he said. 'Won't be a minute.'

'Hang on' said Phil, laughing loudly, 'you wouldn't want to miss anything, would you?'. Twitchett coughed and walked off rapidly. Phil's face wore a very contented smile. He seemed to have been waiting 20 years for this moment. 'Struth. If only you could have been there' he continued. 'That's just what he did then; walked off for a pee and missed the only Cory's Shearwater of the day – at least, the only genuine one. And that's not all he missed.

He paused and sipped at his beer. 'About lunchtime, some other birdwatchers joined us. They were on their way to the Scillies, and had just seen a Long-billed Dowitcher at an estuary down the road. Twitchett decided to go off for it while I stayed behind sea-watching.'

'I can tell you folks it was the worst mistake he could have made. Five minutes after he had gone, one of the other blokes picked up a gull flying north. At first we thought it was an immature Kittiwake, but as it got closer we realised we had a real beaut' – something much rarer than that. Well, I don't have to tell you lot what it was, but it would have made my day, even if nothing else had come along. But a few minutes later, a small skua flew by, quite close in. Pretty small, tern-like flight – you can imagine the excitement. Then, as a sort of grand finale, about half-an-hour later – I guess it wanted to get by before Twitchett got back – the other large shearwater we had hoped to see flew by.'

'Poor Twitchett. It had just begun to rain when he got back. He hadn't seen a sign of the dowitcher, and when the rain started really lashing down we had to retreat to a cafe. He had missed four new birds. It's the only time I've known him not to speak for an hour – until this evening that is.' There was general laughter for a while, mingled with appreciative 'Don't-mind-if-I-do's' as Phil walked to the bar.

'Let me get some drinks in' he said. 'Struth, the beer here's so much better than that stuff in Oz, which tastes like sheer water.' He cackled with laughter at his own joke, while a few groans could be heard from elsewhere in the bar. Nobody noticed Twitchett slipping quietly out of the door.

Phil came back from the bar with a tray of drinks and sat down in Twitchett's chair. It seemed to suit him rather well. Before anyone could object he had pulled out a tobacco pouch and a pipe and, with a dreamy smile on his face, was saying:

'Now this reminds me of an evening in the old George...'

Questions *1. Where were Twitchett and Phil sea-watching? 2. What was the Leach's Petrel that Twitchett claimed more likely to have been? 3. What were the three species that Twitchett missed while he was looking for the dowitcher?*

While spending a spring weekend in Suffolk, Twitchett paid an early morning visit to Minsmere. Here are two pages of the notes he made.

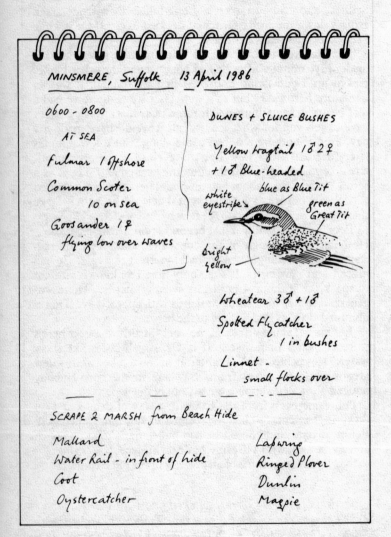

MINSMERE, Suffolk   13 April 1986

0600 - 0800

AT SEA

Fulmar 1 offshore

Common Scoter
        10 on sea

Goosander 1 ♀
    flying low over waves

DUNES + SLUICE BUSHES

Yellow Wagtail 1♂ 2♀
+ 1♂ Blue-headed

white eyestripe →   blue as Blue Tit
                              green as Great Tit
bright yellow

Wheatear 3♂ + 1♂

Spotted Flycatcher
            1 in bushes

Linnet -
    small flocks over

SCRAPE 2 MARSH from Beach Hide

Mallard
Water Rail - in front of hide
Coot
Oystercatcher

Lapwing
Ringed Plover
Dunlin
Magpie

42

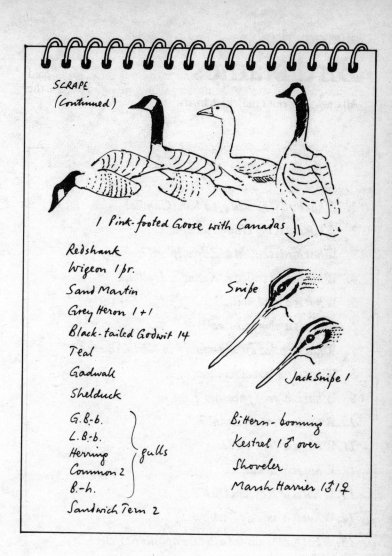

SCRAPE
(Continued)

1 Pink-footed Goose with Canadas

Redshank
Wigeon 1 pr.
Sand Martin
Grey Heron 1 + 1
Black-tailed Godwit 14
Teal
Gadwall
Shelduck

Snipe

Jack Snipe 1

G.B.-b.
L.B.-b.
Herring ⎫ gulls
Common 2
B.-h.
Sandwich Tern 2

Bittern – booming
Kestrel 1 ♂ over
Shoveler
Marsh Harrier 1♂1♀

Question: *1. What three birds did he certainly, or almost certainly, misidentify? 2. What very obvious bird has not been noted by Twitchett?*

Bird Names

All questions refer to British birds.

1. *What bird is named after King Canute?*

2. *What is a King Harry redcap?*

3. *What bird is called a 'Zilpzalp' in Germany?*

4. *What bird is called a 'Kievit' in Holland?*

5. *What is a 'tree mouse'?*

6. *What is a 'flag sparrow'?*

7. *What is called an 'old-squaw' in North America?*

8. *What is an 'eaves swallow'?*

9. *What is a 'reed pheasant'?*

10. *What is a 'sea pheasant'?*

11. *What is a 'fork-tail'?*

12. *What is a 'firetail'?*

13. *What is a 'Royston Dick'?*

14. *What is a 'mizzly Dick'?*

15. *What bird is named after the apostle St Peter?*

16. *What is 'St Cuthbert's duck'?*

17. *What is called a Common Gallinule in North America?*

18. *What is called a 'Bank Swallow' in North America?*

19. *What is a 'mullet hawk'?*

20. *What is a 'bee hawk'?*

21. What is a 'shepster'?

22. What is a 'Margaret's crow'?

23. What is a 'bull of the mire'?

24. What is a 'warden of the marshes'?

25. What is a 'blue woodpecker'?

26. What is a 'blue rump'?

27. What is a 'northern nightingale'?

28. What is a 'nightingale's mate'?

29. What is a 'Joey spodger'?

30. What is a 'mavis'?

31. What is a 'banjo bill'?

33. Give five birds whose names are exact representations (more or less) of their songs or calls.

34. Give three birds or families of birds that are named after the way they fly.

32. What is a 'parrot-billed willock'?

35. What is a 'bud-picker'?

36. What is a 'pickcheese'?

37. What is a 'golden head'?

38. What is a 'red-legs'?

39. What is a 'fern owl'?

40. What is a 'land rail'?

41. What is a 'popinjay'?

42. What is a 'halcyon'?

43. What is a 'moorcock'?

44. What is a 'moor peep'?

45. Give the names of four non-passerines named after their food.

46. Give the names of four passerines named after their food.

47. What is a 'night plover'?

48. What is a 'day owl'?

49. What is a 'shufflewing'?

50. What is a 'ruddock'?

51. What is a 'burrow duck'?

52. What is an 'underground tit'?

53. Give four breeding birds named after people.

54. Give four birds named after places in Britain.

55. What is a 'shoeing horn'?

56. What is a 'broad bill'?

57. What is a 'saw-sharpener'?

58. What is a 'mowing-machine bird'?

59. What is a 'garden ouzel'?

60. What is a 'water ouzel'?

61. What is a 'kitty coot'?

62. What is a 'bare-faced crow'?

63. What is a 'dabchick'?

64. What is a 'bumbarrel'?

"It's either a Hamlyns Little or a Collins Temminck's!"

The Storm

Like most public houses the *Coot and Corncrake* has its quiet nights. In the winter time the darts team takes over on Thursday nights, Mondays are for crib and Tuesdays for dominoes. On Sunday nights the quiz team have their matches, the best attended always being the one between them and the other village pub, *The Black Falcon*.

Wednesdays are always quiet and it was a Wednesday evening in mid December that found Twitchett, Stringwell, Stickler and Listman sat at their usual table by a roaring fire. Outside a gale was blowing and snow had been falling for several hours. With few birds to be seen conversation tended towards stories of birdwatching exploits of the past, a topic which Twitchett needed little encouragement to talk about.

'Mid-December and I'm on 299 for the year' said Stringwell. 'I hope something turns up, I'd hate to be left on that.'

'With the weather as it is at the moment the only thing you're likely to see is an Eskimo Curlew.'

'Some hope' said Stringwell, 'they're nearly extinct. Hardly anyone sees them in the States these days.'

'Last British record was in 1887 on the Scillies' said Listman. 'I bet they used to get some other real cripplers there in those days.' He sighed and stared at his empty glass.

'Funny you should mention extinct birds' said Twitchett, 'it reminds me of a story my great grandfather used to tell.'

'Runs in the family' whispered Stickler to Stringwell.

'It was in weather just like this' began Twitchett, ignoring them. 'I'm sure I've mentioned that old Peregrine Twitchett was something of a traveller. There was nowhere he hadn't sailed in search of birds. Well it was the spring of 1912. He was sailing to New York, on the way to the funeral of his brother Eustace. Did I ever tell you how he died?'

'Frequently' mumbled Stringwell.

'Anyway somewhere past halfway they hit a storm. Hurricane force winds, snow and feezing temperatures. Needless to say the boat foundered and capsized. Peregrine was lucky enough to jump into a life-boat just before the calamity. He drifted for days, keeping himself alert by writing a diary. He saw Killer Whales, sharks and even a couple of icebergs. At one point he saw a large boat on the horizon, heading west. It was a huge steamer with four funnels, but it was too far away to see him. Days and days he was adrift, until suddenly he saw some birds, Gannets to be precise, diving for food. The sight of them brought new hope. They were adult birds and he knew that he must be near land. Sure enough he could see a small island in the distance and as luck would have it the life boat drifted towards the rocky shore.' Twitchett coughed at this point and placed his empty tankard on the table noisily.

'Sorry Twitchett,' said Stringwell who had appeared to be dropping asleep. 'It's the fire, it makes me drowsy. I'll get some drinks. Another round please Rossie' he said, walking towards the bar.

'Now where was I?' said Twitchett, when Stringwell had returned. 'Ah, yes. The island.' He sipped at his beer. 'Well Peregrine made it ashore and was able to secure the boat in a small cave. There was a narrow rocky shore around the island and above this towered sheer rock faces, over hundreds of feet high. Peregrine could see that ledges on the cliff face were crowded with seabirds, so many that their droppings fell on him like steady rain. The life-boat had contained some useful items to help him survive but unfortunately these did not include climbing equipment or an umbrella.

He made the cave he had found his base, managing to find enough driftwood to build a small fire. Food was his main problem. It was present in abundance on the cliff ledges where every seabird imaginable was breeding. On the ledges were Guillemots, Razorbills, Fulmars, Gannets, Cormorants, Kittiwakes, Black-headed Gulls and Herring Gulls. The grassy top appeared to be the home of Puffins, Storm Petrels and Manx Shearwaters and he watched them flying up to their breeding burrows.

Like all Twitchetts, Peregrine was well endowed with physical courage, as well as a good head for heights. And in the course of his many travels, had become an accomplished climber. Unfortunately, despite all his efforts, the cliffs were so steep that there was no way to get at the enticing store of food he could see around and above him. The only thing he did have was a small revolver in his pocket, which he had always carried on his foreign trips ever since he and his brother had to

fight their way out of a Indian ambush using nothing but a dissection kit and a telescope. They don't make telescopes like that these days you know.'

'Never could trust them' said the Colonel from his stool at the bar

'What, telescopes?' asked Twitchett, glaring at him.

'No, Indians,' answered the Colonel. 'Always had reservations about them. Ever since 1932 when they started playing in the Test.'

Twitchett continued regardless. 'Peregrine fired off a few shots at passing gulls but soon realised it was futile. In desperation he began to explore what he could of the island, which wasn't much when the tide was high although he was able to scramble over some of the surrounding rocks. Anyway, to cut a long story short...'

Stringwell grunted loudly.

'..to cut a long story SHORT.' repeated Twitchett, starting to get a little annoyed with interruptions from his usually attentive audience.

'One morning while exploring he suddenly came face to face with a sight he could not believe. Standing on a rock not 50 yards from him was a PENGUIN! Well at first he thought it was a penguin, it was the right shape and size, black and white, what else could it be. Perhaps it had escaped from a zoo or a circus, like the tiger which killed his brother. Did I ever...'

'YES' came a loud chorus from the table, waking up the Colonel who thought they were all out.

'Well it wasn't until his brain cells had undergone a rapid readjustment that he realised it was a Great Auk. A species that was supposed to be extinct. Not seen for 70 years. And here was one stood right in front of him. Peregrines head began to swim. His name would become famous worldwide. This was better than any of the new birds he had found in the past. Headlines in the newspapers... it was the thought of newspapers that did it. Their association with fish and chips, I suppose, but suddenly Peregrine felt very, very hungry. This bird represented salvation in both an ornithological and ornithivorous sense. His mind in a turmoil, Peregrine got out his revolver, checked it was loaded and... While making these preparations the bird had disappeared. Peregrine ran to the rock where it had been stood, but there was no sign of it. He searched the surrounding rocks without any success and on returning to the original position of the bird he noticed a cavity in the nearby rocks. On inspecting it he found a large eggs, about five inches long, white in colour with some darker streaks and spots. Clearly it was the egg of the bird he had seen. He took the egg back to his cave and stared at it for hours. If he ate it, what evidence would there be for its existence. But if he carefully cracked it and kept the shells... He described the resulting omelette as 'a rich yellow colour, tasting strongly of fish and rotting seaweed'.

'Sounds like one of Rossie's pies' whispered Stickler, laughing.

'He never saw the bird again,' continued Twitchett, 'and after eating the last of the omelette he set off in the lifeboat again and was eventually picked up off the coast of the Outer Hebrides. Peregrine was quite delirious when he was found, or so his rescuers thought. His perpetual babbling about escaped circus animals and omelettes were taken as the sign of a deranged mind and he spent the next two years in a quiet sanitorium near Hastings.

The only evidence of his discovery, the eggshells, had all disappeared and the notebook he wrote in during the ordeal makes no mention of the island, although the last few pages were irreparably damaged by seawater. He had spent a total of 26 days at sea.

His description of the island is rather vague and no-one has proven its existence. It was after hearing the story that poor old Featherstone got it into his head to go and search for the island. He visited St Kilda, North Rona, and Sula Sgeir. It was on his visit to Rockall that he fell to his death. He was flown out to the island and managed to climb down to the shore. It was on his way back up that he slipped and fell. He was seen on the shore beforehand waving madly and jumping up and down, but he was rather like that, poor chap.'

Twitchett knocked out his pipe and got up. 'Well I think I'll head for home now. The storm seems to have blown over and all this talking has made me hungry. Anyone like to come back for a bite?'

'What are you having' asked Stringwell.

'I don't really know, but I quite fancy an omelette' said Twitchett, smiling.

Questions: *1. 1. Which seabird was clearly misidentified by Peregrine? 2. Which seabirds is he unlikely to have seen? 3. Why was Peregrine lucky not to have been picked up by the liner?*

Folklore, Music and Literature

1. Which bird reputedly tried to draw the nails from Christ's cross?

2. Which bird reputedly tried to remove the thorns from Christ's crown of thorns?

3. Who composed On hearing the first cuckoo in spring?

4. According to the poet William Blake, what 'puts all heaven in a rage'?

5. Who wrote The Birds, *a play first produced in 414 BC?*

6. Who wrote the book on which Hitchcock's film The Birds *was based?*

7. What bird is represented by the oboe in Prokofiev's Peter and the Wolf?

8. Who compared the clamour of the Trojan host to the noise of migrating cranes?

9. Who was the bird-god of ancient Egypt?

10. Who composed The Lark Ascending?

11. What bird's song did Shakespeare describe as 'word of fear, unpleasing to the married ear'?

12. Of which bird did Browning write 'he sings his song twice over'?

13. What bird did Thomas Hardy describe as having a 'crocus coloured bill'?

14. To whom did Alice confess that she ate eggs?

15 *In* Babes in the Wood, *which bird covers the children with leaves?*

16. *Gilbert White wrote 'The uncrested wren... has only two piercing notes.' What is the bird?*

17. *What bird does John Clare's 'The March Nightingale' describe?*

18. *Which bird 'sat on the Cardinal's chair'?*

19. *Which bird's beak can 'hold more than its belly can'?*

20. *'In April come he shall, In May he sings all day.' What is he, and what does he do in June?*

21. *Ben Jonson likened Shakespeare to which bird?*

22. *Which bird will 'sit in a barn and keep himself warm, when the north wind doth blow'?*

23. *What three birds can be heard in Beethoven's Pastoral Symphony?*

24. *What French song describes the plucking of a Skylark?*

25. *What bird sits on the shoulder of Athene (Minerva)?*

26. *What bird did Zeus become in order to seduce Leda?*

27. *About which club did Arthur Ransome write his* Swallows and Amazons *books?*

28. *What bird did Robert Burns describe as 'the blitter frae the boggie'?*

29. *Who killed cock Robin?*

30. *Who wrote the opera* Le Rossignol?

31. *Who wrote 'He clasps the crag with crooked hands' and about which bird?*

32. *Who quoth 'Nevermore', in a poem by which author?*

33. *Who wrote the tale* The Emperor and the Nightingale?

34. *What bird 'lays its eggs in a paper bag'?*

35. *Who wrote an 'Ode to a Nightingale'?*

36. What bird served as a croquet mallet in Alice in Wonderland?

37. Who described which bird in a poem beginning 'Hail to thee blithe spirit'?

38. In the children's song, which bird 'sat in an old gum tree'?

39. What bird is supposed to have started the Hundred Years War?

40. What bird did Hamlet know a hawk from?

41. What bird did Wordsworth describe as 'ethereal minstrel'?

42. What bird is a symbol of longevity in China and Japan?

43. Who composed 'Hark, hark the lark'?

44. What British satirist had a bird's name?

45. What bird said 'Pieces of eight'?

46. In Paradise Lost Milton describes Satan as 'Sat like a …' what?

47. What bird rises from its own ashes?

48. In the Last Tournament Tennyson refers to a 'yaffingale'. What bird is it?

49. Haydn's Symphony No 82 in F minor is known by which bird's name?

50. Who composed the 'Firebird'?

51. Who composed 'Tit Willow'?

52. From the haunts of which birds does Tennyson's brook 'make a sudden sally'?

53. Who wrote 'He thought he saw an albatross that fluttered round the lamp.'?

54. What 19th Century novelist had a bird's name?

55. What bird features in the title of a book by Harper Lee?

56. What birds 'came up at even and covered the camp'?

57. Who composed 'The Golden Cockerel'?

58. Who composed 'The Thieving Magpie'?

59. What was the name of Dr Dolittle's parrot?

60. According to fable, which bird sat on the eagle's back and then flew higher than him?

61. What birds saved Rome?

62. What bird brings luck if it nests on your roof?

63. Who said 'What a beautiful pussy you are'?

64. Who wrote, and in what, 'She laments, sir, her husband goes this morning a'birding.'?

News of a Rough-legged Buzzard at Benacre in Suffolk drew Twitchett there last winter. Uncharacteristically, he failed to see the buzzard, but here are a couple of pages of his notes of what he did see.

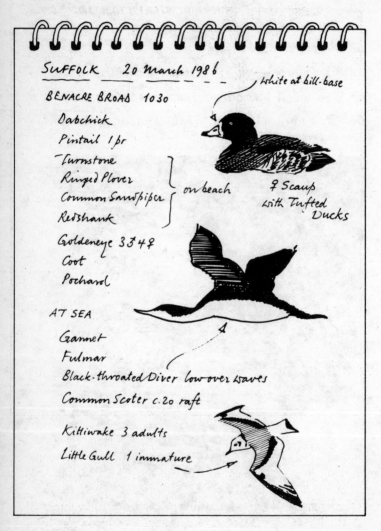

SUFFOLK   20 March 1986

BENACRE BROAD   1030

Dabchick

Pintail 1 pr

White at bill-base

Turnstone
Ringed Plover   on beach
Common Sandpiper
Redshank

♀ Scaup
with Tufted
        Ducks

Goldeneye 3♂ 4♀

Coot

Pochard

AT SEA

Gannet

Fulmar

Black-throated Diver low over waves

Common Scoter c.20 raft

Kittiwake 3 adults

Little Gull 1 immature

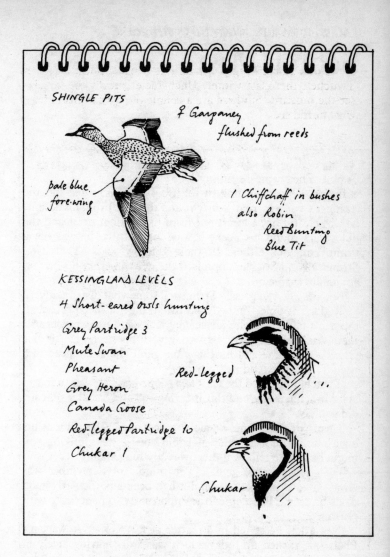

SHINGLE PITS

♀ Garganey
flushed from reeds

pale blue
fore-wing

1 Chiffchaff in bushes
also Robin
Reed Bunting
Blue Tit

KESSINGLAND LEVELS

4 Short-eared owls hunting
Grey Partridge 3
Mute Swan
Pheasant
Grey Heron
Canada Goose
Red-legged Partridge 10
Chukar 1

Red-legged

Chukar

Questions: *1. What was the rarity Twitchett misidentified?*
2. What were the other three birds that he identified wrongly?
3. Which bird would not count on his year list?

Scotch Mist

'A pint of heavy please Jimmy.'

It was a quiet evening in the *Coot and Corncrake* and the stranger's voice carried clearly round the bar. From his accent, he was clearly not a local; but from his outdoor dress and the binoculars round his neck, it was obvious that he was not a stamp collector either. In their window seats, Twitchett, Stringwell and Stickler appraised the newcomer with a certain amount of suspicion.

'Sounds like a jock' said Stringwell somewhat disparagingly.

'Right first time, Jimmy' said the stranger as he approached the trio's table. Despite his shaggy locks and unkempt beard, there was evidently nothing wrong with his hearing. 'Alastair Goatit's the name and birding's ma game' he announced in a friendly voice, extending his hand.

'Twitchett' replied the *Coot and Corncrake*'s answer to Baron von Munchhausen, 'and this is Stringwell and Stickler – Goatit did you say?'

'Goatit in one, Jimmy' said the Scotsman, chortling at his own joke. 'You'll no mind if I join you? I was thinking you might be able to tell me if there was anything about?'

Twitchett became genial. The middle of September was always a good time of year and it had been a particularly good day's birding. He accepted the opportunity to pontificate with relish.

'Not a lot' he stated in a matter of fact voice. 'A Wilson's Phalarope turned up today and it was still showing nicely in front of the hide this evening, but at the moment, apart from half-a-dozen Little Stints, nine Curlew Sandpipers, a couple of Greenshank, a few Ruff, a Whimbrel, several Spotted Redshank and the two Pectoral Sandpipers that have been around for a few days, it's been fairly quiet on the wader front for our little patch.'

Stringwell had caught Twitchett's quick wink but Stickler, momentarily distracted by an extremely tight t-shirt bearing the words 'Birdwatchers do it in Sandy Beds' had not, and was looking distinctly puzzled. He started to remind Twitchett that only half-an-hour earlier he had been describing the day as a 'real cracker'. But his puzzled look turned rapidly to one of pain as he was cut short by the impact of Stringwell's boot against his shin.

Ignoring Stickler's winces, Twitchett continued. 'Definitely worth taking a walk out to the point' he said. 'I had a Red-breasted Flycatcher and a couple of Yellow-browed Warblers in the bushes near the Coastguard Station this afternoon, and there had obviously been a fall as there were a lot of Robins and Pied Flycatchers around as well. Coming back along the path by the wood, a Red-backed Shrike sitting on a fence post was also a new arrival and I was almost home when I flushed a couple of Short-eared Owls. Altogether quite a fair day, I suppose. Hardly outstanding, but then we're rather spoiled by good birds in this part of the world.'

'Sounds like a real cracker to me' said the Scot, evidently impressed. 'We dinna get birds like that on ma local patch.'

'Where exactly is your local patch?' enquired Twitchett.

'I'm from Aviemore' replied the Scot. 'So I suppose you'd say Speyside was ma local patch. We may not get some of your birds, but I don't expect you get many Golden Eagles, Ptarmigan and Crested Tits down here very often'. 'A highlander, eh?' mused Twitchett, in his 'I've just thought of a story' voice. 'I've always liked your part of the world. Famous for its birds and... 'he paused as he held out his glass of malt in a silent toast '...its whisky and... ' he paused again '...of course famous for its mysteries.' There was a gleam in his eye at the last few words.

'Och, aye, there's a lot of folk would give their right arm to ken what's hiding in the depths of Loch Ness' said Goatit.

'Indeed' continued Twitchett 'but as it happens, it wasn't to that particular mystery that I was referring. No, the mystery that I was thinking about is one that none of you here may have heard of. It concerns the giant bird of Glen Griffinroch.'

'Cannae say I've heard of that' confirmed the Scot.

'You soon will' said Stringwell and Stickler in unison as Twitchett began the familiar ritual of filling his pipe.

'It was back in April '71 that it happened' said Twitchett. 'I was on my annual trip to pick up all the Scottish 'goodies' and after three days on the west coast I had already seen well over 100 species. In one spot I even had Choughs mobbing a Golden Eagle while a party of Barnacle Geese flew by. An amazing sight! In Speyside, of course, I went to see the Ospreys and from the hide I also had a fantastic view of Crested Tits, Scottish Crossbills and a party of Siskins. Soon after that, I was wandering around the forest trying to locate a Lesser-spotted Woodpecker I'd heard drumming, when I almost walked into a magnificent male Capercaillie which took great exception to my presence and started to scuttle after me with alarming speed. For such a large bird, I wouldn't call a caper slow.'

'The last night of my trip was to be spent at Glengriffinroch Lodge, the home of a distant and aging relation of mine, one Ranald MacCrearity. A bit of a birder in his time by all accounts, the old boy was now not only extremely partial to a drop of the malt but, as they say up that way, he was also "not the full shilling." '

'A boozy old nutcase, you mean', said Stickler with a sidelong glance at the Colonel.

Twitchett frowned. 'Accurate if somewhat tactless' he replied. 'Rumour had it that the old boy's condition had been caused by the sighting of some fearful and monstrous bird many years before, but nobody in the family ever discovered the full story.'

'Under normal circumstances I wouldn't have chosen to stay with him but I had been intrigued by his cryptic invitation, which had informed me that he "wished to tell me something before he went", and as family stories had always suggested that he wasn't short of a bob or two, I couldn't really refuse. Glen Griffinroch, which lies somewhere south-west of Kingussie on the road to Loch Laggan, was remote to say the least, and by the time I eventually arrived, Ranald was in no state to tell me anything. According to his manservant, Angus, he had opened a bottle of 12-year-old to celebrate my arrival, but after one or two drams he had apparently got a taste for it, and the empty bottle and the comatose figure of Ranald were all that remained of the reunion party.'

'With conversation unlikely until the following morning, I sought Angus's advice, and 20 minutes later I was striding through the heather en route to the Glengriffinroch Arms. It was a pleasant half-mile or so across the moor, with Ring Ouzels, Wheatears and Red Grouse everywhere, and the track took me close to a small lochan where I saw a pair of Red-throated Divers, resplendent in their breeding plumage.'

'A good record, that' remarked Goatit, 'they don't usually come that far east.'

'Well, they were definitely Red-throated' retorted Twitchett rather brusquely, as if his identification were being questioned. 'Now, where was I?'

'Just about to reach the pub and buy a drink' replied Stringwell, placing his empty mug on the table in a rather obvious fashion.

'All right, all right, get them in' said Twitchett in a resigned voice, and threw a five-pound note at Stringwell.

A few minutes later, their glasses replenished, Twitchett's audience was back in attendance.

'As I reached the place' he continued, 'I noticed that the sign depicted a huge bird of sorts, but it looked as though the painter had taken considerable artistic license and, to be honest, I didn't really give it a second thought. The inside of the place looked like a set from Brigadoon, and although the locals were friendly enough, there was a strange atmosphere that I couldn't explain. They were particularly interested in my binoculars and, after a good few malts, a youngish man called Dougal with fiery red hair asked me if I had "come for the bird". My immediate thought was that there must be something about locally – a breeding Grosbeak or something like that – but that line of thought was soon dispelled when Morag, the barmaid, told Dougal to "Hush man, the gentleman's no wanting to hear your fanciful tales tonight." Try as I might, I could get nobody in the bar to tell me anything more and, as the time passed and the whisky flowed, the incident passed from my mind.'

'It was well after midnight before I eventually decided that I would have to get home. The bagpipes were playing and it looked as though the locals were in for a long night as I headed towards the door. "Mind and keep to the path, now" shouted Dougal as I went out into the night. For the first few hundred yards, I made good progress, despite the dark. It wasn't long, however, before I somehow lost the path and was suddenly stumbling about in the heather.'

'You were sozzled' said Stringwell.

'I most certainly was not' said Twitchett emphatically, and carried on hastily with his story. 'It was at that point that I first heard the wailing. Eerie, mewing wails that seemed to fill the air. I was pretty shaken, I can tell you, but with typical Twitchett resolve I pressed on through the heather.'

'Pretty obvious what the wailing was, I'd have thought' whispered Goatit to Stringwell, but Twitchett was by now so involved in his tale that he failed to notice the interruption.

'Before long' he went on 'I found myself beside a little stand of pines. I had just paused to get my breath back when there was suddenly this tremendous flapping noise as a gigantic bird came out of the trees.'

'Oh come on Twitchett' said Stickler in a tone of disbelief. 'Let's face it: you were out of the box. It was probably just a flock of Woodpigeons you heard.' Twitchett began to go his well-known purple colour.

'I was not drunk I tell you' he shouted. The bar went very quiet and Twitchett had to attend to his pipe for quite some time before he regained his composure.

'I have to admit that the noise gave me a nasty turn' he continued, 'but just minutes later, as I was descending a steep slope, things got even worse. Suddenly there was a loud whooshing noise above my head, and something seemed to hit me in the back. I was aware of a huge beak and glaring eye, and then I was tumbling down the bank and everything went black. I must have been knocked out.'

Stickler looked as though he was about to say something, but sensibly refrained.

'Then what happened' demanded Goatit.

'Luckily' continued Twitchett 'in falling, I had actually ended up on the path again, and once I had come round, it didn't take me long to get back to the house. The next morning, I had rather a sore head, but apart from that and a few bruises, I appeared to be relatively unscathed. My hopes of questioning Ranald about the previous night's events were soon dashed when Angus revealed that he had had a quick pick-me-up before breakfast and had forgotten to stop. I decided that it was time to leave.'

'I was just about to go when I discovered that I had lost mu car keys. The place where I had fallen seemed the obvious place to look and so I set off to try to find it. Despite the darkness of the night before, I located the spot without any difficulty and, astonishingly enough, I found the keys almost at once. It was just as I was turning to go that I saw the feather.'

'Wait... no, don't tell us' mocked Stringwell. 'It was about two feet long?'

'Wrong' retorted Twitchett. 'It was more like five feet!'

'This is getting ridiculous' exclaimed Stringwell.

'It was a dark chocolate-brown colour with a very black tip' boomed Twitchett, oblivious to all comments 'and I was just about to pick it up when...'

'You woke up?' suggested Stringwell.

'WHEN... a sudden and inexplicable gust of wind blew up,

lifted up the feather and carried it out into the bog, where it sank slowly without trace.'

'How convenient' said Stringwell. 'Well, Twitchett, I have to hand it to you. You've really got quite an imagination.'

'Imagination, eh?' said Twitchett. 'Then perhaps you can explain this'. Carefully, he laid a faded old photograph in the centre of the table. Despite the quality of the print, there was no mistaking the gigantic size of the feather that lay beside Twitchett's binoculars in the Scottish heather.

'My God' said Stringwell, beginning to colour.

'I thought you'd be tickled pink by that' said Twitchett. Mine's a large malt.'

Questions: *1. What bird did Twitchett misidentify in the story? 2. Where did Twitchett see the Choughs, Barnacle Geese and Golden Eagle? 3. What was making the wailing that Twitchett heard on the moor?*

A MYSTERY

In the course of preparation of this book, by means that we are not at liberty to divulge, the editors chanced to come across some curious correspondence. While it would be too much to say that these papers – when pieced together from the rather tattered state in which they were received – confirm Twitchett's account of his unhappy Scottish experiences, as related in the preceding pages, they do nevertheless lend a certain credence to his claims. The reader must form his or her own judgement.

Telephone: 01-493 7070

Telegrams: Herakles, London W1X
Telex: 25611 Collins G

Collins·Publishers

8 GRAFTON STREET. LONDON W1X 3LA

30 July 1986

Norman Arlott Esq.
Hill House
Tilney St Lawrence
Norfolk

Dear Norman,

NEW GENERATION GUIDE: BIRDS

Here are the four plate~
as ma~'`

...ked on the overlays ... ...s that need slight changes, soon as possible?

I wonder if you could help me with your advice on another matter. I'm painting a series of panels for the Wildfowl Trust, for a display at Arundel, showing six famous wetlands in different parts of the world. One of them portrays Lake Nakuru in East Africa, and I want to centre the composition on a flock of Ostriches pitching in to land. I seem to be having difficulty in finding references to help me in this, and I've never myself seen Ostriches in the wild. I know that you're familiar with the species, and so I'd be most grateful if you could have a look at the accompanying sketch, and let me have your comments.

Love to Marie and your other handmaidens ...

Yours ever,

Crispin

Crispin Fisher
Natural History Editor

Hill House,
School Road,
Tilney St. Lawrence,
Near King's Lynn,
Norfolk.

Telephone: 0945 880543.

5 August 1986

Dear Crispin

Please find enclosed the four corrected New Generation Guide plates.

It was also good to see your preliminary sketches for your hide panels depicting Lake Nakuru. Before advancing with this however, I feel you really should check on the way the Ostrich carries its neck whilst in flight – you have made the common error of confusing the flight character of the Cassowary with that of the Ostrich – see enclosed my own sketches.

Also, watch those hind toes!

All in all I think, when correct, the final painting will enliven many a birding outing to Sussex.

All best wishes.

Norman.

Norman Arlott

Flying Ostrich or Cassowary.

From own notes
lake Natron.

Taken from live programme
on Radio 4 — Living World.

Cautionary note. *While not questioning the authenticity of these sketches, the editors admit to a feeling of unease. There is, they feel, something not quite right about them. The question is, what is it?*

Record Breakers

Questions 1 to 37 refer to British birds, those from 38 to 64 to the whole world.

1. *Which is the heaviest British bird?*

2. *Which is the lightest British bird?*

3. *To which species does Britain's longest-lived individual bird belong?*

4. *Which British bird has the longest tail?*

5. *Which is the heaviest British breeding warbler?*

6. *Which is the heaviest British passerine?*

7. *Which is the most widespread British breeding bird?*

8. *Which is the second most widespread British breeding bird?*

9. *Which is the most widespread summer visitor to Britain?*

10. *Which is the heaviest British breeding finch?*

11. *Which is the heaviest British breeding duck?*

12. *Which is the most widespread British breeding wader?*

13. *Which is the most widespread British bird of prey?*

14. *Which British passerine lays most eggs in a single clutch?*

15. *Which British bird dives deepest under the water?*

16. *Which British bird dives longest under the water?*

17. *Which British bird has the most broods in a year?*

18. *Which British bird forms the largest flocks?*

19. *Which British bird has the highest pitched call?*

20. Which British bird has been recorded as having the most fledged young in a single year?

21. Which British bird has the lowest pitched call?

22. Which British bird has the longest incubation period?

23. Which British bird has the shortest incubation period?

24. Which British bird spends the highest proportion of its life on the wing?

25. Which British breeding bird has the longest legs in proportion to its total length?

26. Which British breeding bird has the longest wing in proportion to its bill-tail length?

27. Which British breeding bird has the longest bill?

28. Which British breeding bird has the longest bill in proportion to its body length?

29. Which British bird has the highest annual mortality rate?

30. Which British bird takes longest to achieve maturity?

31. Which British bird breeds at the highest altitude?

32. Which British bird builds the biggest nest in proportion to its size?

33. In which British species is there the greatest discrepancy in weight between the male and the female?

34. Which British bird has the widest field of vision?

35. Which summer visitor spends the shortest time in Britain?

36. Which is usually the earliest warbler to arrive in Britain?

37. Which of the families that include a British breeder contains the fewest number of species altogether?

38. Which is the heaviest bird in the world?

39. Which is the lightest bird in the world?

40. What is the longest known movement of an individual bird?

41. Which is the most numerous bird in the world?

42. Which is the most numerous seabird in the world?

43. Which bird has the largest wingspan?

44. Which bird makes the longest regular migration?

45. Which bird has the longest wingspan?

46. Which bird has the longest bill?

47. Which bird has the longest incubation period?

48. Which bird lays most eggs in a single clutch?

49. Which is the fastest flier?

50. Which is the heaviest flying bird?

51. Which bird has been recorded at highest altitude on land?

52. Which bird has been recorded at highest altitude in the air?

53. Which is the smallest owl?

54. Which bird builds the biggest nest?

55. Which birds occupy the most populous communal nest?

56. Which is the family whose eggs are most nearly spherical?

57. Which bird has the fastest wingbeat?

58. Which bird has been seen nearest to the South Pole?

59. Which wild bird has the longest feathers?

60. Which is the most geographically widespread family of land birds?

61. Which country has the highest number of breeding species?

62. Which family contains the most species?

63. The members of which family spend the longest periods without resting on land?

64. What is the oldest living family of birds?

The Tree

To the casual observer, the bar of the *Coot and Corncrake* appeared fairly busy. To the trained eye of a regular, however, one feature was immediately noticeable and that was the absence of Twitchett and Stringwell. Normally that would only mean one thing – a bird, some wind-blown rarity, that was keeping them from their usual places by the window. Only the true regular would realise that it was the first Friday in December, the evening of which was always reserved for a strangely ritualistic event – Twitchett's annual 'dinner'.

It had all started one night when someone had decided to challenge Twitchett's seemingly unlimited capacity for telling tall stories. It was suggested that there must be a topic about which he would be unable to talk. Twitchett rapidly proved otherwise and so enjoyed himself, as well as entertaining everyone present, that he decided to make it an annual event. He proposed a dinner at which he, Stringwell, Listman and other specially invited guests would attend.

A strict format was laid down for the occasion. It would always be the first Friday in December and would naturally take place at the *Coot and Corncrake*. A dinner was arranged in the back room of the pub and the guests would assemble there at 7 o'clock. One of the group had the task of finding a suitable topic, this job rotated each year but somehow never fell to Twitchett. The topic was announced at the beginning of the meal and after the meal each person, except the one who thought of the subject, had to tell a story. For the first few years the group had stayed within the back room but after persistent complaints from other regulars who wanted to hear the stories, they now moved through to the bar after the meal.

This year Twitchett had invited his friend Ackroyd to join them and had asked him to find a topic. At half-past-six they were all gathered in the bar having a preliminary drink before adjourning for the meal.

'I've got an interesting topic for you all' said Ackroyd. 'I've tried to find one that will restrict Twitchett's well-known love of exaggeration, not to mention downright lies.' They all laughed as Twitchett nearly choked with indignation.

'Lies?' he boomed. 'I never lie. All the stories I tell are true.'

Loud throat-clearing noises greeted this statement and Twitchett began to turn purple.

'Let's all go through to the back room' said Ackroyd anxious to prevent Twitchett performing his infamous impersonation of Etna erupting.

They all filed through and sat at their marked places at the table. Ackroyd stood up and cleared his throat.

'Before I tell you tonight's topic I will just remind you of the rules. Each story must last for a minimum of ten minutes and a maximum of twenty. There must be no interruptions during the story. Any comments must be reserved until the end. The stories must be entertaining, factual and in no way must they be inflammatory.'

Everyone at the table nodded, they were all familiar with the rules.

'I will give you the topic in a moment and you will think of your stories during the dinner. At an appropriate time we will return to the bar where story-telling will commence.'

'Come on man,' growled Twitchett. We all know the rules. Give us the Subject.'

Ackroyd smiled and cleared his throat. 'Tonight's topic' he said, as if announcing an item on 'Twenty Questions' . 'Tonight's topic is "My favourite tree." '

A groan came from Stringwell. 'What sort of a topic is that?' he asked.

'You can be the first to tell us' laughed Ackroyd. 'Listman can be next and then Twitchett.' He smiled strangely in Twitchett's direction.

The dinner was, as ever, superb. Rossie had prepared his usual comic menu. Mulligatawny (owl) soup, followed by Rollmop heron, Roast Mother Carey's Chicken, Goose Berry Fool, Black-winged Stilton, coffee and liqueurs. One year he had prepared a buffet but this had not been repeated as Stickler had complained that the dips provided were a personal dig at him.

It was now about half-past-eight. Everyone had finished and moved through to the bar. Drinks were passed round and Stringwell began to tell his story.

It was not one of his best. He told about a large old oak tree he knew. How he had climbed it as a boy, the nests he had found and the birds he had seen there. A nice little story but not exceptional. A round of applause came at the end of it, waking up the Colonel who, thinking he was at Lord's, shouted 'Howzat.'

It was now Listman's turn. No-one had any doubt that his tale would be embellished with his usual meaningless statistics.

'My favourite tree' he began, 'is my family tree.' He winked at Ackroyd and all eyes turned to Twitchett. Smiles went round the room as everyone thought that he must have stolen Twitchett's thunder, for nobody liked talking about their forebears more than he did.

Listman told of his grandfather in Greece, his aunt in Austria, his niece in Nicaragua and his cousin in the Seychelles. All of them had some link with the birds in the countries they inhabited. He told of each of their lists, what percentage of each country's birds they had seen. He finished by asking which bird appeared on all of their lists. At the end of his tale their were murmers of appreciation and loud applause.

'I liked the bit about your aunt and her yodelling to call out a Three-toed Woodpecker.' said Twitchett. 'It reminds me of one of my relatives...'

'Is this relevant to your story?' asked Ackroyd.

'No.' said Twitchett, 'But I thought that..'

'It's your turn now' said Ackroyd firmly.

All eyes and ears, except for the Colonel's perhaps, were focussed on him.

He sat back in his chair and lit the pipe he had just filled. He took a few puffs and as the smoke was clearing he began.

'The story I am about to tell you concerns a most singular tree, I believe a Norway Spruce. It was probably about 100 years old when I first saw it, and was about 80 feet high. It had a good complement of wildlife associated with it. Coal Tits and Goldcrests nested in it, Mistle Thrushes and Greenfinches roosted in it and Treecreepers and woodpeckers would feed from its trunk and branches.'

'The first good bird I saw in the tree was a Red-breasted Flycatcher, perched on one of its branches one September. Since then I have seen over 70 species in it.'

'I then went abroad and didn't see the tree for many years. On my return I found it was a shadow of its former self. It had lost many branches and I could only see one nest, belonging to a crow. It had not, however, lost its attraction for birds.'

Twitchett paused at this point and got another drink. He

had a quiet, confident smile on his face and we all knew that he was readying himself for the final assault.

'That autumn there was a tremendous storm with howling north-easterly winds. The tree swayed about like a drunken sailor.' Twitchett paused at this point for refreshment.

'The following day there were birds everywhere. Redstarts, Blackcaps, Blackbirds and Golcrests were present in good numbers. The best birds were two Yellow-browed Warblers which were feeding in the tree and a Wryneck I disturbed which flew up into it. In the afternoon the warblers were still there but the Wryneck had gone, being replaced by a Red-backed Shrike. The same storm was obviously the reason for the appearance of some other strange birds which I happened to see while sitting in the shade of the tree. The first of these was a Gannet, closely followed by two Arctic Skuas, and then, most incredible of all, a Red-billed Tropicbird.'

'Come off it' said Stringwell, 'that's not on the British list. These stories are supposed to be true.'

'This is all quite true' said Twitchett, his eyes twinkling with delight. 'The tropicbird flew past about 50 yards away, I could see its bill and tail quite clearly.'

'The next time I saw the tree was a few years later, in the spring this time, just after some strong south-westerlies. Heavy rain overnight had obviously brought down some migrants. A couple of bedraggled Willow Warblers sat on a branch, preening. A bee buzzed past my head and suddenly something black and white flew out, caught it and flew into the tree. It was larger than a sparrow and its crown colour identified it immediately.' He looked at Stringwell and Ackroyd who were both nodding and had clearly worked out what it was.

'As it was about to eat the bee the warblers suddenly dived for cover with a cry of alarm as a bird of prey flew over. It was large, almost Peregrine size, but it was all dark, its yellow feet showing clearly as it tried to grab one of the little birds.'

'That's ridiculous' said Listman. 'There have only been a couple of records, and they were in the west. Where is this tree of yours anyway?'

'No interruptions' shouted Twitchett, banging his tankard on the table so hard that his pipe jumped out of the ashtray and onto the floor, breaking it's stem. He took his spare pipe out and began to fill it, staring at Listman with steely eyes.

'Now where was I' said Twitchett. 'Had I got to the Blue-cheeked Bee-eater?'

Stringwell choked on the mouthful of beer he was drinking

and started coughing so loudly that the Colonel shouted 'Mustard Gas! On with your masks.'

'The bee-eater I just mentioned appeared later in the day,' continued Twitchett, 'marvellous male it was. It provided some competition for that nice black and white beast. A few more birds were perched up in the tree. An Ortolan Bunting even flew down and started to pick at the remains of my lunch. Anyway, just as I thought I'd seen everything the sky suddenly darkened and a Griffon Vulture...'

'That's it' said Stringwell. 'I can't accept this. You've gone right overboard this time.'

Suddenly Twitchett began to laugh. It was a small chuckle at first but rapidly grew into a full blown fit that came close to hysteria. Tears were running down his face. He had to take his pipe from his mouth and accidentally placed it in his tankard instead of the ashtray which caused him to laugh even more. His face had become bright purple and his breath was coming in short bursts.

'I can't carry on' he said in between bouts of laughter. 'That last comment of yours was so true, Stringwell. Thats exactly what I did do three days later.' He guffawed even louder and gasping for air staggered to his feet and made for the Gents.

A stunned silence was left. Suddenly Stringwell's face broke into a smile. 'Of course' he said. 'It's obvious.' And he too started laughing.

Ackroyd was clearly totally lost by these outbursts. 'I don't understand what's going on.' he said.

Stringwell leaned over to him. 'The tree... ' he said, with tears of laughter beggining to appear in his eyes. 'The tree, don't you see? It's a... ' His last word was blotted out to all but Ackroyd by the timely ringing of Rossi's bell for last orders which coincided with Twitchett's return to the bar. He could hear laughs as Stringwell's discovery was passed round. Exhausted yet jubilant he returned to his chair, sat back and began to dry out his pipe.

'It was strange you should have mentioned yodelling' he said to Listman. 'It reminds me of a similar tale. It all began with some bagpipes...'

Questions: *1. What bird could all of Listman's relatives have seen? 2. What was Twitchett's tree? 3. What was the identity of the black and white bird? 4. What was the bird of prey Twitchett saw?*

Distribution

Questions 1-24 refer to British birds, the remainder to Europe.

1. What are the four introduced waterfowl that so far breed only in England?

2. What two other introduced species breed only in England?

3. Which two birds of prey breed only in England?

4. Which four waders breed only in England?

5. Which four warblers breed only in England?

6. What are the other six birds (all passerines) that breed only in England?

7. Apart from the irregular Redwing, what are the three passerines that breed only in Scotland?

8. Which two game birds breed only in Scotland?

9. Which three waders breed only in Scotland?

10. Which entire family is confined to Scotland for breeding?

11. What are the other four birds that breed only in Scotland?

12. Which is the seabird whose only English breeding site is in Cumbria?

13. Which grebe breeds furthest north in Britain?

14. Of which two species of geese do two separate subspecies come to Britain for the winter?

15. Which British breeding owl was introduced?

16. Which are the only eight warblers that breed in Eire?

17. Which European-breeding sawbill does not breed in Britain?

18. Which true tit does not breed further north than Edinburgh-Glasgow?

19. Which bird breeds in England but nowhere else in Europe?

20. Which bunting breeds in all mainland European countries but not in Britain?

21. Which is the only gull that breeds exclusively in England?

22. What three birds breed only on Scottish islands?

23. How many geese are summer visitors to Britain?

24. Which British breeding chat does not breed in Scandinavia?

Questions 25-64 refer to Europe.

25. In which country is the northernmost breeding Alpine Swift?

26. In which country is the northernmost breeding Rook?

27. In which country is the southernmost breeding Arctic Skua?

28. In which country is the southernmost breeding Rook?

29. In which country is the southernmost breeding Crested Tit?

30. Which European country has no breeding Dunnock?

31. Which European country has no breeding Starling?

32. Which are the only two European countries with no breeding Redshank?

33. Which are the only two European countries with no breeding woodpeckers of any species?

34. In which European country is the Kestrel exclusively a summer visitor?

35. In which European country does Sanderling breed?

36. In which European country are there no breeding members of the snipe family at all, not even Woodcock?

37. In which European country does Black-winged Pratincole breed?

38. In which European country do Mediterranean Gulls but not Black-headed Gulls breed?

39. In which European country does Iceland Gull breed?

40. In which European country does White-rumped Swift breed?

41. In which European country is the Swallow the only breeding Martin?

42. In which European country does Firecrest but not Goldcrest breed?

43. In which European country do Marsh Tits but not Willow Tits breed?

44. In which European country do House, Italian, Spanish, Tree and Rock Sparrow all breed?

45. In which European country does Grey Plover breed?

46. Which four birds are confined to Europe?

47. In which two European countries does Blackcap but not Garden Warbler breed?

48. In which country do Spoonbills breed nearest to Britain?

49. Where is the breeding place nearest to Britain of Whooper Swan?

50. In which country is the breeding place nearest to Britain of Scaup?

51. Which is the only mainland European country with no breeding kingfisher?

52. Which is the only mainland European country with no breeding Black Woodpeckers?

53. Which is the only grebe to breed in Iceland?

54. Which coastal country between Finland and France has no breeding Rock Pipits?

55. Which is the only shearwater to breed in Norway?

56. Of which two goose species has Britain the only resident European breeding populations?

57. Which four vultures breed in Europe?

58. Which bird of prey's breeding range in Europe is confined to the Mediterranean?

59. Which warbler breeds in Iceland?

60. Which warbler has the smallest European breeding range?

61. Which warbler has the most widespread European breeding range?

62. Which true thrush breeds in Iceland?

63. Which finch breeds in Iceland?

64. Name the five birds that breed regularly in every single European country (including Iceland)?

"According to this we shouldn't be here at all!"

The Party

Christmas was drawing near again. Rossie, the landlord of the *Coot and Corncrake*, had arranged the customary extension on Christmas Eve and conversation was now turned towards the forthcoming festivities.

'I think we should have a session of charades' said Stickler, who had always fancied himself as a bit of an actor.

'No, I don't think so' said Twitchett, 'remember the last time we played that. The Colonel was given Black-capped Chickadee to mime and he spent the next half an hour trying to persuade us that W.C. Fields never wore a black cap.'

'How about birdsong imitations?' suggested Stringwell.

'As long as we give you Mute Swan', said Listman, 'you had the RSPCA round here last year with your Water Rail.'

'It will have to be "Guess what bird you are" again' said Twitchett, smiling to himself. This was a game at which he excelled. He had never been beaten in 15 years and had got his identity each time in the lowest number of questions.

'I thought it would be back to that again' said Stringwell, 'but we'll make sure to get you this time.'

So Christmas Eve arrived. The *Coot and Corncrake* was

decorated with baloons and streamers. Someone had put a paper hat on the Colonel who appeared to be quite oblivious to its presence.

The game was due to start at ten o'clock. All the regulars from the pub had contributed half a dozen bird names and these had been written on labels which could be stuck on a person's back. Rossie put all of these into a hat and drew one at random for each player. Thus a person might be given one of their own suggestions without knowing it. The game was then quite simple. Players took it in turns to ask the others questions and from their yes or no answers they must guess the bird name on their back. Invariably everyone started with 'Am I a passerine?' or 'Am I British?' and then it gradually became more difficult. You were allowed two guesses at your identity and it was another boast of Twitchett's that he had only ever needed one guess.

So at 10 o'clock the labels were pulled out of the hat and stuck on; 36 labels had been prepared and all but 11 of them were used.

Stringwell was a Needle-tailed Swift which took him 15 questions. Listman was a Resplendent Quetzal which took him 18 questions and two guesses. The Colonel, who insisted on playing was given Hutton's Vireo and fooled everyone with his first question 'Do I play for England?'.

By tradition the defending champion's turn came last and Twitchett Knew that to retain his title he must not only guess right first time, but only had 14 questions.

With the utmost confidence he stood up, knocked out his pipe and began. He had no way of knowing whether it was one of his own suggestions that he had been given as only four of his six had been used. From the standard of the others he knew he was in for a tough time.

'Do I breed in Britain?' began Twitchett. 'No' came the reply.

'Have I been seen in Britain?' Again 'No.' He frowned and took a pipe cleaner from his pocket and began to clean his pipe.

'Am I found elsewhere in Europe?' A third negative.

'Am I found in Asia?' 'No.'

Four questions so far and Twitchett had very little information. One year he had taken nine questions to establish the country of origin of an Emperor Penguin.

'Am I North American?' 'Yes.' Bingo, the first clue. Now it should be easy. 'Am I a passerine?' 'No.'

Now it became a bit more tricky. Without realising he was

doing it Twitchett had taken his now severely tarred pipe cleaner and was stirring his beer with it.

The choice of questions had become crucial. It was a North American non-passerine, but which family?

'Am I a Charadriiform?' asked Twitchett, and to his surprise got the answer 'Yes.' With a sigh of relief Twitchett removed the slightly cleaner cleaner from his beer and sucked it. With a look of sheer horror he began coughing and spluttering. He grabbed for his beer to wash the taste away, only making things worse. It took three mouthwashes with Famous Grouse to calm him down.

Twitchett had now asked seven questions and had reduced the field to nine families. He resumed the game.

'Do I have webbed feet?' A ripple of laughter went around and someone shouted 'Why, are you at sea then Twitchett?' The reply to Twitchett's question was another 'Yes.'

Now it was a toss up. Gulls, terns, skuas or auks. Wait a minute, don't forget skimmers. If in doubt go for the obvious thought Twitchett.

'Am I a gull?' Affirmative.

Now Twitchett felt himself to be on solid ground and there were five more questions to go.

'Have I got a black head?' he asked and then cursed himself. 'No' came the expected answer.

Four questions left and Twitchett was beginning to sweat. He ordered another pint and then sat down, nervously playing with a pipe-cleaner.

'You'll never do it' said Stringwell, who was the current leader. But Twitchett didn't hear him. He was deep in thought with images of American gulls flying around his head. Suddenly an inspiration. Yes, that was just the sort of bird they would pick.

'Have I got red legs?' 'No' came the answer, amidst hoots of laughter as people tried to look under Twitchett's table.

Twitchett was feeling distinctly hot under the collar. He poked out his pipe, realising suddenly that he'd only filled it a few minutes ago.

'Have I got... ' he began, but then stopped, shaking his head. He could hear the blood pounding in his ears. His palms were sweating and he couldn't seem to focus his thoughts.

'Have I got a red bill?' again the answer 'No.'

Twitchett had a look of total concentration on his face. His eyes were tight shut and he was muttering quietly to himself. Occasionally words like California and Canada could be heard.

Finally he opened his eyes and asked 'Do I breed on the west coast?' 'No.'

'Do I have black on the wing?' Again 'No.'

'I've got it for sure' said Twitchett smiling. 'I'm a Thayer's Gull.' He sank to his chair, still red in the face, and appeared to be visibly shaking.

'I'm sorry, you're wrong' said Rossie with a huge grin. Twitchett's face went through a complex change of colours. First it went bright purple and then became blotchy, finally settling for off-white. His pipe, which he had just re-lit, fell from his mouth onto his lap. His head fell forward and shook from side-to-side. 'I couldn't have been anything else,' he kept muttering.

'All right' said Rossie. I think we've played him along for long enough. 'You've been had, Twitchett, my old friend.'

'What?' said Twitchett, looking up, not really understanding the comment.

'We have all been fooling you. You didn't really fail, although you didn't guess the right bird, but that's hardly surprising.'

'I don't know what you mean.' said Twitchett. 'How were you having me on?'

'Well we all agreed to play a trick on you' explained Stringwell. 'We told everyone in the pub about it so you can blame us all. The trick was quite simple. Every time you asked a question, if the right answer was 'Yes', we said 'No' and vice-versa. We thought you would catch us out well before you got to the stage of guessing.'

'Just to be fair we won't count your last guess, but if you can remember the questions and answers you should easily be able to work out what you really are.'

So after a couple of minutes Twitchett told them what he really was. He also told them what they all were, in no uncertain terms, although even he agreed that it had been a good evening's game. 'A cruel trick to play on me, though' said Twitchett. 'Which reminds me. Did I ever tell you the story about my cousin Gertrude and the quail's eggs...'

'Time, please' shouted Rossie, 'and a Merry Christmas to you all.'

Questions: *1. What was Twitchett's real identity? 2. Why was one of Twitchett's questions wasted? 3. If Twitchett had been given the answer 'Yes' to his question about red legs, what might his guess have been?*

Only Ones and Odd Ones Out

The first 32 questions all refer to British birds.

1. Which is the only wader with a crest?

2. Which is the only bird that climbs down tree trunks?

3. Which is the only woodpecker with identical males and females?

4. Which is the only gamebird with identical males and females?

5. Which is the only wader with three toes?

6. Which is the only gull with three toes?

7. Which is the only accentor to breed in Britain?

8. Which is the only British crow that doesn't breed in England?

9. Which is the only duck with a summer and winter plumage?

10. Which is the only duck that is a summer visitor to Britain?

11. Which is the only finch with identical males and females?

12. Which is the only bunting with identical males and females?

13. Which is the only owl to breed in Britain and the Falklands?

14. Which is the only wader to breed in Britain and the Falklands?

15. Which is the only tit to excavate its own nest hole?

16. Which is the only passerine to feed underwater?

17. Which is the only wader with red eyes?

18. Which is the only wader with yellow eyes?

19. Which is the only passerine with feathered feet?

20. Which is the only pigeon with a white rump?

21. Which is the only tit that doesn't breed in England?

22. Which is the only tit that occurs as a vagrant?

23. Which is the only breeding pipit with black legs?

24. Which is the only breeding lark with dark legs?

25. Which is the only crossbill that hasn't bred in Britain?

26. Which is the only breeding passerine with an all white head?

27. What are the only three breeding passerines with yellow in their outer tail feathers?

28. Which is the only bird with a red bill with a yellow tip?

29. Which are the only two breeding passerines with decurved bills?

30. Which is the only bird with a black bill with a yellow tip?

31. Which is the only breeding bird with a white bill?

32. Which is the only bird to moult its bill?

Odd Ones Out: Possible answers to many of these questions may be that only one bird is a migrant, a passerine or a non-passerine. While these answers would be correct, they are not the answers being looked for. The question in each case is 'Which is the odd one out and why?'

33. Gannet, Rook, Starling, Sandwich Tern.

34. Grasshopper Warbler, Dunnock, Cuckoo, Kittiwake.

35. Arctic Tern, Tufted Duck, Cormorant, Little Grebe.

36. Cetti's Warbler, Blackcap, Reed Warbler, Dartford Warbler.

37. Hen Harrier, Wheatear, Yellowhammer, Bullfinch.

38. Goldeneye, Great Spotted Woodpecker, Shelduck, Blue Tit.

39. Avocet, Chaffinch, Marsh Tit, Common Tern.

40. Kittiwake, Black-headed Gull, Red Kite, House Martin.

41. Tufted Duck, Coot, Short-eared Owl, Stone-curlew.

42. Manx Shearwater, Leach's Petrel, Fulmar, Storm Petrel.

43. Gull, Tern, Sandpiper, Grebe.

44. Shoveler, Common Scoter, Shelduck, Mute Swan.

45. Dunnock, Meadow Pipit, Reed Warbler, Yellow Wagtail.

46. Blue Tit, Long-tailed Tit, Great Tit, Coal Tit.

47. Herring Gull, Lesser Black-backed Gull, Common Gull, Great Black-backed Gull.

48. Black Guillemot, Raven, Puffin, Chough.

49. Redstart, Dunnock, Song Thrush, Starling.

50. Whinchat, Woodchat, Stonechat, Rock Thrush.

51. Little Bittern, Nutcracker, Pallas' Sandgrouse, Bee-eater.

52. Red Grouse, Black Grouse, Capercaillie, Ptarmigan.

53. Tufted Duck, Ruddy Duck, Ferruginous Duck, Bombay Duck.

54. Nightingale, Sandpiper, Kestrel, Owl.

55. Long-tailed Duck, Blue Tit, Starling, Bar-tailed Godwit.

56. Pied Wagtail, Garden Warbler, Cirl Bunting, Redstart.

57. Snipe, Great Spotted Woodpecker, Tree Pipit, Whitethroat.

58. Yellowhammer, Cirl Bunting, Snow Bunting, Reed Bunting.

59. Grouse, Snipe, Kite, Wagtail.

60. Treecreeper, Great Crested Grebe, Curlew, Chough.

61. Ringed Plover, Skylark, Sand Martin, Shelduck.

62. Ringed Plover, Skylark, Sand Martin, Common Tern.

63. Grey Heron, Coot, Blackbird, Starling.

64. Gannet, Osprey, Sandwich Tern, Kingfisher.

The Mathematician

The usual local customers were in the bar of the *Coot and Corncrake* on this particular Sunday afternoon. The Colonel was sitting on his stool by the bar and Twitchett was in his favourite chair by the window with Stringwell, Stickler and Listman. The topic of conversation was the current Test Match against India, and the failure of the England team to cope with the fast bowling.

'Some of these Indian chappies are rather swift' said Twitchett.

'I remember that' barked the Colonel, 'caught on the boundary by mistake. Or was it a swallow?'

'Don't tell me the batsman got a duck' joked Listman.

'Must have been luck' muttered the Colonel and downed his gin and tonic as a chuckle of laughter came from the group.

'Talking of swifts' said Twitchett 'did I ever tell you the story about the bird's-nest soup? Well, it all began when I was out east. I always like to muck in and go for the local dishes.' Stringwell winked at Listman.

'I was in this little restaurant one day when I spotted a strange parasite floating on the surface of my soup. I immediately realised that it was unlike any that had been seen before and must therefore have come from the nest of a bird that was hitherto unknown to science. I called the waiter over to ask him where it had come from and he, thinking I was complaining about it, promptly removed the bowl of soup and dashed off with it. Threw the whole bally lot away and I never found another like it.'

Conversation stopped momentarily as the door opened and all eyes were turned on the stranger who entered. He was dressed as a typical outdoor type, with large khaki shorts, open-neck shirt, strong walking boots and socks nearly up to his knees. He was tall and his balding head, domed forehead and thick glasses gave him the appearance of a serious studious fellow. He glanced around him as though taking careful note of his surroundings before going up to the bar and demanding a half of shandy. As the buzz of conversation began again, he seemed to become involved in an altercation with Rossie on the subject of his change.

'Going back to the subject of cricket' said Listman, grateful for the intrusion of the stranger and hastily taking the opportunity to change the subject, 'there is a high probability that the outcome of the series will be a win for England. Looking at the statistics over the last 50 years...'

'I always get confused with all these statistics they throw at you' interrupted Twitchett. 'Batting averages, bowling averages, number of maidens...'

'I remember a number of those' mumbled the Colonel, 'dashed pretty all of them.'

'How do they work it out?' asked Twitchett. 'Last week, two of our bowlers each had an average of 12, one getting five wickets for 60 runs and the other getting three for 36. That was the first innings. Now in the second innings they both got a single wicket for 24. So their averages should be equal on 18. Then the old commentator, Brian West or whoever it is, says that the first bowler has an average of 14 and the second 15. It doesn't make sense.'

'Statistically it does' said a voice from the bar. Everyone turned to the tall bespectacled stranger who appeared to have completed his financial negotiations. 'The first bowler was more consistent in the first innings and so his average works out lower. You get the actual figure by adding the runs and wickets for the two innings together and then working out the average. Another half please.'

There was a period of silence until Twitchett looked at him with eyes narrowed. 'You don't look like a cricket commentator, how do you know about these things?' he asked.

'You're correct about my not being a commentator' said the stranger. 'In fact I'm a mathematics lecturer at Imperial College. Angler's the name, W.R. Angler

Again there was a period of silence, the locals rather resenting this intrusion and not quite sure what to say to him anyway.

'How did your day go yesterday, Twitchett?' asked Stickler, desperately trying to change the subject away from anything to do with cricket or maths.

'Oh, pretty well considering the weather' answered Twitchett, getting out his notebook and settling back into his chair. 'Of course the rain in the early morning didn't help so I

concentrated on woodland birds to begin with. Managed to get all three woodpeckers quickly, although I only heard the Green Woodpecker drumming. Tree Sparrow took a little finding, as did Corn Bunting. The old Tawny Owl was in his usual spot, he was my 50th bird of the day, but I couldn't find a Little Owl. However I did have one stroke of luck before the morning ended.' He paused to fill his pipe.

'Hang on while I get a drink' said Stringwell, 'a pint for all of you?'

'Yes please' said Twitchett, 'and a box of matches.' There was a longish pause while Stringwell ordered and paid for the drinks, during which the stranger pointed out that he had been under-charged for his round. Rossie was looking decidedly bemused and started pressing keys on the till in a rather distracted fashion. Eventually Stringwell returned and Twitchett continued.

'While it was still raining, I decided to cut my losses and go straight down to the hide by the marsh where at least I could keep dry. As soon as I opened the flap I saw it, feeding at the edge of the pool. It had a long bill and was probing into the mud. Its legs were short and it appeared brown all over but it was difficult to tell as the visibility was terrible with the rain pouring down. Then, just as I got my binoculars, on it a harrier flew over and scared it off.'

'Marsh or Hen?' enquired Stickler.

'Jump-jet actually' said Twitchett, rather annoyed at the interruption.

'As I was saying. I only saw the bird briefly but was able to identify it immediately as a Great Snipe, a species that I have intimate knowledge of, having watched them on their breeding grounds in Denmark. Of course I dashed out of the hide to see where it had gone and watched it flying off far into the distance.' He paused again, this time to light his pipe.

'But how did you manage to watch it fly into the distance if the visibility was that bad?' asked Stickler. Twitchett was not to be deterred.

'After lunch the weather began to clear. I had seen 16 species of waders on the marsh by the time I left, which left me on 75, well down on previous years. I headed for the local heathland where Stonechat was easy, so was Tree Pipit and a lark flew over which could only have been a Wood Lark. A quick trip down to the coast then for a few gulls and terns on the 'patch' by the power station, where I also saw a distant Gannet. Not a bad day all things considerd although not as good as my May 1st twitches in the past. I can still remember the day I had in 1978, when...' He began to look nostalgic.

'How many did you see in the end?' asked Listman hastily.

'Well,' said Twitchett, with a touch of regret, 'I saw 32 species less than last year when I thought I was going to break 150. It's all in my notebook, along with my list for last year.' He pointed to the book which Listman picked up.

'Now that's interesting,' he said. 'Both last year's total and this year's total are each prime numbers.'

'In that case' said the stranger, 'your total this year was...'

'Last orders' shouted Rossie, ringing the bell and drowning out the answer.

Questions: *1. How many species had Twitchett seen this year? 2. What two mistakes were there in his description of the birds he saw? 3. Why would the Great Snipe have been particularly unusual; what was it more likely to have been?*

Miscellany

All questions refer to British birds.

1. Which bird used to nest in colonies of 30 square miles or more in area?

2. Which bird arrived back in Britain with the Falklands Task Force?

3. In falconry, which bird would be used by an emperor?

4. In falconry, which bird would be used by a knave?

5. Which bird colonised the London bomb sites in the 1940s?

6. What sort of birds are caught in decoys?

7. Where do flamingos get their pink colour from?

8. Where was Scotland's first bird observatory?

9. How many passerine species are there in the world; 3,000, 5,000 or 7,000?

10. Edinburgh Zoo has a free-flying population of which bird?

11. The down of which bird would be used to stuff the pillows of St Kildans?

12. Which single bird 'doesn't make a summer'?

13. People are described as 'As proud as ...' which bird?

14. Which English football team is known as 'The Canaries'?

15. What is a Caracara?

16. Name four British finches with white rumps.

17. Which bird has once nested in Britain on St Giles' Cathedral, Edinburgh, in 1416?

18. Which British tern has a yellow bill with a black tip?

19. Which American baseball team is known as 'The Cardinals'?

20. Which British bird has bright red underparts and a yellow crown?

21. Where are the only Ivory-billed Woodpeckers known to be?

22. Where does the Muscovy Duck originate?

23. Which English football team is known as 'The Owls'?

24. Which birds were parachuted into German-occupied Europe during World War 2?

25. Where was Western Europe's first bird observatory?

26. What is a brolga?

27. Which birds, according to Ogden Nash '…lead Bohemian lives, they fail as husbands and as wives'?

28. Which is the only bird whose upper mandible is shorter than its lower?

29. Aylesbury ducks are descended from which wild bird?

30. What is a dowitcher?

31. What birds are collectively known as a 'muster'?

32. In which American state do Great Northern and White-billed Divers both breed?

33. Which American baseball team is called the 'Orioles'?

34. Which is the only European Heron with different male and female plumages?

35. What bird might have put a jinx on you?

36. What is a Jabiru?

37. What is a Maribou?

38. Which gull is all-white with black feet and a dark yellow-tipped bill?

39. What two races of the Bluethroat occur in Britain?

40. How many birds would the beloved have received by the end of the 12th day of Christmas?

41. What birds nested in Edward Lear's Old Man's beard?

42. Which of the birds in the previous answer might really nest in Old Man's Beard (or Clematis vitalba)

43. How many birds of prey regularly breed in Britain?

44. Which British bird has sails on its wings?

45. Which wader breeds in every one of the United States, excluding Hawaii?

46. Which two birds of prey breed in every one of the United States?

47. How many feathers are there on a humming bird; 1,000, 2,000 or 3,000?

48. What two Welsh football league teams have birds' names?

49. Which adult British gull has an all-black underwing?

50. What have a lark, eagle and treecreeper got in common?

51. What bird spent many years on the Bass Rock, and can now be seen at Hermaness in Shetland?

52. How many birds are there on the British List, to the nearest ten?

53. What bird is associated with cider?

54. What bird might you associate with Flaubert?

55. Who was Jonathan Livingstone?

56. What ornithological connection is there with the Barclaycard?

57. What did 'one fly over'?

58. Who said 'I'll dig his grave'?

59. Which is the odd one out: Lochwinnoch, Loch of the Lowes, Loch Garten, Loch of Kinnordy?

60. Which of these birds would Sweeney Todd not be interested in: vulture, tern, sparrow, warbler?

61. What bird was recently introduced to the island of Rhum?

62. Who sang 'Ride a white swan'?

63. What hit did Fleetwood Mac have with a bird?

64. What is the connection between Jenny Agutter, Paul Gallico, Richard Harris and Peter Scott?

It is Whitsun, and Twitchett has temporarily deserted the *Coot and Corncrake* to take a holiday in the Camargue. These are some of the notes he made on the trip.

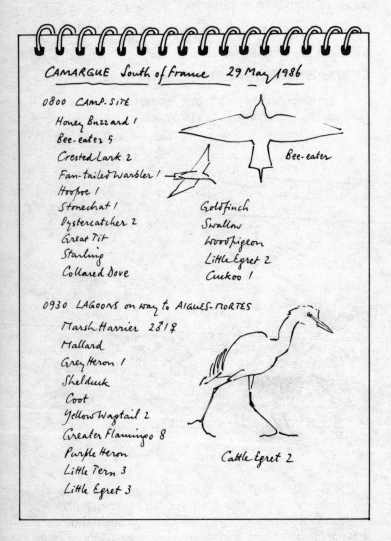

CAMARGUE   South of France   29 May 1986

0800 CAMP. SITE

Honey Buzzard 1
Bee-eater 5
Crested Lark 2
Fan-tailed Warbler 1
Hoopoe 1
Stonechat 1   Goldfinch
Oystercatcher 2   Swallow
Great Tit   Woodpigeon
Starling   Little Egret 2
Collared Dove   Cuckoo 1

Bee-eater

0930 LAGOONS on way to AIGUES-MORTES

Marsh Harrier 2♂ 1♀
Mallard
Grey Heron 1
Shelduck
Coot
Yellow Wagtail 2
Greater Flamingo 8
Purple Heron
Little Tern 3   Cattle Egret 2
Little Egret 3

Reed Warbler
Canada Goose
Tawny Pipit

Gull-billed Tern 1

1145 TRACK to woods, back of camp

Lesser Grey Shrike 2
Rook
Jackdaw
Crested Lark
Bee-eater 3
Buzzard 1

Hoopoe 2
Treecreeper
Cetti's Warbler
Nightingale
Melodious Warbler 1
Roller 1

1400 COAST at LES SAINTES-MARIES

Eider 5
Herring Gull
   (yellow-legged race)
Lesser Black-backed Gull
Med. Gull 1 imm.
Little Gull 5
Sandwich Tern 3
Slender-billed Gull 1

Avocet 2
Bar-t. Godwit 1
Marsh Harrier 2 ♂
Black Kite 3
Whimbrel

Questions: *1.Which two birds* couldn't *have been there, and what were they really? 2. Which two birds* shouldn't *have been there, and what were they more likely to have been? 3. Which bird did Twitchett presumably imagine?*

Colour Quiz

These questions all refer to adult males in spring unless they state otherwise.

1. What colour is a Goldfinch's rump?

2. What colour is a Yellowhammer's rump?

3. What colour is a Little Egret's feet?

4. What colour are a Greylag Goose's feet?

5. What colour are a Coot's eyes?

6. What colour are a Common Gull's eyes?

7. What colour is a Pheasant's bill?

8. What colour is a Red-legged Partridge's bill?

9. What colour is a Blue Tit's forehead?

10. What colour is a Pied Wagtail's forehead?

11. What colour is a Grey Wagtail's throat?

12. What colour is a Sand Martin's throat?

13. What colour is a Gannet's tail?

14. What colour is a Fieldfare's tail?

15. What colour is a Wheatear's back?

16. What colour is a Chaffinch's back?

17. What colour is a Starling's egg?

18. What colour is a Woodpigeon's egg?

19. What colour is a juvenile Blackcap's crown?

20. What colour is a juvenile Bullfinch's crown?

21. *What colour is a Woodpigeon's breast?*

22. *What colour is a Pochard's breast?*

23. *What colour are the outer tail feathers of a Blue Tit?*

24. *What colour are the outer tail feathers of a Great Tit?*

25. *What colour is a Black-headed Gull's head?*

26. *What colour is a Kestrel's head?*

27. *What colour are the secondaries of an Avocet?*

28. *What colour are the secondaries of a Goldfinch?*

29. *What colour are the underparts of a House Sparrow?*

30. *What colour are the underparts of a Bee-eater?*

31. *What colour is a female Green Woodpecker's crown?*

32. *What colour is a female Goosander's head?*

33. *What colour is a Redpoll's chin?*

34. *What colour is a Jay's throat?*

35. *What colour is a House Sparrow's forehead?*

36. *What colour is a Swallow's forehead?*

37. *What colour is a Chaffinch's rump?*

38. *What colour is a Twite's rump?*

39. *What colour is an Eider's tail?*

40. *What colour is a Nightingale's tail?*

41. *What colour are a Tufted Duck's eyes?*

42. *What colour are a Woodpigeon's eyes?*

43. *What colour is a Blue Tit's back?*

44. *What colour is a Bullfinch's bill?*

45. *What colour is a Mallard's bill?*

46. *What colour is a Starling's bill?*

47. *What colour are a Cuckoo's feet?*

48. *What colour are a Puffin's feet?*

49. *What colour are a Blue Tit's eggs?*

50. *What colour are a Song Thrush's eggs?*

51. *What colour is a female Marsh Harrier's crown?*

52. *What colour is a female Blackbird's bill?*

53. *What colour is a Dunnock's breast?*

54. *What colour is a Grey Wagtail's breast?*

55. *What colour is a Shoveler's head?*

56. *What colour is a Grey Partridge's head?*

57. *What colour is a juvenile Goldfinch's face?*

58. *What colour is a juvenile Great Spotted Woodpecker's crown?*

59. *What colour are a Great Crested Grebe's secondaries?*

60. *What colour are a Woodpigeon's secondaries?*

61. *What colour are the underparts of a Blue Tit?*

62. *What colour are the underparts of a Hooded Crow?*

63. *What colour are the outer-tail feathers of a Yellow Wagtail?*

64. *What colour are the outer-tail feathers of a Magpie?*

The Celebrity

For a Wednesday night at 7 o'clock, the *Coot and Corncrake* was remarkably busy. But then it wasn't every day that the village played host to 300 birders, various technicians and broadcasters from the BBC and – the focus of all the attention – a bird of such rare quality.

It all seemed to have happened remarkably fast. The bird had first been seen early that morning. It was certainly recorded at an early hour by young Bob Spottiswood (known to all and sundry as 'Spottit'), but there were some mysterious and conflicting stories about the initial sighting which have still never been satisfactorily resolved. 'Spottit' was 15, a pimply and bespectacled youth, but he probably knew more about the marsh then anybody, including Twitchett. And his habit of getting in a couple of hours birdwatching before school meant that he was often out and about well before the rest of the birding community. When not out on the marsh or at school he could often be seen around the village doing odd jobs to earn a penny or two, because his family were not well off and it was well known that he earnestly desired a decent pair of binoculars to help him with his birdwatching.

Young 'Spottit' knew his birds, however, and within ten minutes he was confident that what he could see in front of him was pretty spectacular. He had still been writing his copious field notes from the hide, when Listman had appeared. He had made the statutory enquiry 'Anything about?', and had initially seemed highly sceptical about the answer he was given. Appearances, however can be deceptive: after checking through his own, rather fine, pair of binoculars, he had remarked in an extremely casual voice 'Ah, that. Saw it on the way over. Of course. I meant anything else interesting about?' Shortly after that he had said something about an urgent appointment in the village, and left. By mid-morning, the grape-vine was well and truly buzzing. By lunchtime, most of the locals had 'had it' and the tills of the *Coot and Corncrake* were already ringing merrily. And by tea-time, the swelling ranks had been joined by a regional television news team from the BBC. At that stage, the discovery and identification seemed to have been attributed to Listman.

Presenting the story was none other than 'Mr Countryside' himself – the famous author, naturalist and one-time cricket commentator, now mainly known for his Radio programme 'Nature Today', He had just happened to be in the regional office when the news broke, and had insisted on covering the story himself. For many casual onlookers, this 'guest' appearance was more exciting than the bird itself. Listman had been in his element:

'Twenty-eighth British record; first for the county' he expostulated with authority to the celebrated man.

The cameras whirred, the buxom young production assistant tried in vain to spell 'palearctic' and young Bob 'Spottit' stood disconsolately by, like the boy whose father monopolises the train set on Christmas Day. For once in his life, even Tom Stickler had contrived to get there in time and, in a frantic effort to publicise this fact to the world, he spent the entire interview trying to get himself into the frame. Later, back at the studios, his antics had so driven the editor to distraction that he had eventually dispatched virtually all trace of the unfortunate 'Dipstick' to the cutting room floor – only the briefest glimpse of a woolly hat was allowed to remain.

Evening had fallen early on the marsh on that late March afternoon, and as the light went so, apparently, did the star attraction. Small parties of latecomers, anxious and out of breath were told 'Showing well an hour ago, but it looks as though its gone now', said in the smug tone of voice of those who know they won't have to return again at dawn.

By 7 o'clock that evening, the *Coot and Corncrake* was well and truly packed. Rossie had installed a television (temporarily) in the place normally occupied by Twitchett's great-grandfather's Whip-poor-will, so that all could watch when the moment finally came for the village to be broadcast to the world.

'Haven't known an evening like this since the Eye-browed Thrush' confided Rossie to the distinguished visitor, popping another fiver into the till. It had certainly been a remarkable day.

Perhaps the most remarkable fact, however, was that no-one had seen Twitchett. His usual chair remained empty, save for the Barbour jacket that Stringwell had draped across it. It was going to be bad enough as it was, but if Twitchett couldn't get his seat as well...

'Better not rub it in when he appears' Stringwell said to Stickler and Listman.

'As if we would.' Stickler grinned smugly, blissfully un-aware that his only chance of a television appearance now lay in an outtake for 'It'll Be All Right On The Night'. 'Actually, I would have rung and let him know, but I assumed that Listman had already done it, didn't you Stringwell? I say, you did give him a call, didn't you Listman?'

'Er, ah' grunted Listman, who appeared to be rather dis-tracted by the sight of young Bob 'Spottit' making a 'phone call in the corner. 'Must pay a visit to the gents' he said hurriedly, and heaved himself from his seat.

The hubbub in the bar increased as the time for the broad-cast approached. Tantalising snatches of conversation could be heard drifting through the air.

'... very crow-like' a male brown jersey opined to a female blue cagoul.

'... reminded me of a Green Woodpecker... ' his companion seemed to be replying.

From over in the corner, near where Listman and 'Spottit' were in deep and rather heated conversation, a cider-drinking, sub-adult grey windcheater was heard to offer '... rather tern-like, I would have said.'

Even the Colonel, on his usual stool by the bar, could be heard barking 'Hutton, it must have been. Missed them both, by jove. Hah!' The celebrity who was gesticulating into the Colonel's hearing aid was wearing a puzzled and rather hunted expression.

Listman by now was back in his seat, having finished his conversation with 'Spottit', who had taken to peering intently out of the window – no doubt in the hope of catching some nocturnal rarity. 'Still no sign of Twitchett?' he enquired, looking rather pale after the excitement of the day and fiddling listlessly with his nearly empty glass. 'Not like him to be late. Is it one of his days for a trip to that 'cousin' of his in town?'

'I suppose it might have been' said Stringwell. His car had certainly gone when I drove past his house this morning, and that usually only happens when he has to go to town.'

'Probably on one of his solo trail-blazing exercises again' said Listman dismissively.

'Well, he'll certainly be blazing when he gets back' con-tributed Rossie, as he cleared part of the growing graveyard of empty glasses, including Listman's, from the table. 'I just can't remember when Twitchett last missed a 'first' for the marsh – and a first for the county at that.'

'Never' boomed the unmistakeable voice of the man himself, who was standing magisterially at the door. Oddly, he was dressed in an old-fashioned double-breasted suit, but this in no way detracted from the shock his sudden appearance caused. Rossie was so startled that he went into a sudden spasm, cascading glasses and generous quantities of dregs into Stickler's lap.

'Hell's Bells, Twitchett, you didn't half give me a turn' he complained. 'Well, I take it you've heard?'

'Of course I've heard, you bunch of weasels' said Twitchett. 'But not as soon as I would have liked.' He scowled accusingly at the trio at the table, who began to cower, imagining the wrath to come. To their relief, however, the beginnings of a smile began to appear on Twitchett's face. Stringwell was quick to seize the opprtunity.

'Have a drink, he said. Listman's round. Pint, is it? We saved your seat.'

'Bitter... and a whisky' said Twitchett, looking rather pleased with himself. He left the doorway and strode to his seat. Few people noticed the slight figure of 'Spottit' sidling in directly after him; Twitchett was, as usual, the centre of attention. Even the celebrity at the bar, by now escaped from the Colonel's attentions and correcting his production assistant's spelling with great attention, looked up to see what was going on.

Meanwhile Listman was looking strangely agitated. 'Funny' he said. 'I could have sworn I had some money on me. Can any of you chaps lend me a fiver?'

'Not me' said Stickler quickly. 'I've only just got enough to see me through.'

'Nor me' said Stringwell. 'I've got to pay the milkman in the morning, or there'll be hell to pay.'

They fell silent. All eyes were on Twitchett, who was normally well equipped with money. Twitchett, however, was looking very uneasy. 'Most peculiar' he said, patting his jacket pocket with a flapping hand. 'Heavy day. Must have been more expensive than I thought.'

Stringwell gave in. 'Oh well' he said resignedly. 'The milkman will have to wait again. I'll get them in.

'Actually' he said, returning with the drinks, 'we just didn't know where you were. You didn't need it did you? You must have seen plenty in your time.' He almost sounded as though he were feeling sorry for Twitchett. He needn't have worried.

'Dozens' replied Twitchett, sipping contendedly at his whisky. 'Spain, Portugal, south of France – all the usual places – and, of course, I saw the Humberside long-stayer in '82.'

'It might appear again tomorrow' Stringwell suggested hopefully.

'Probably dead already' said Listman dourly. 'You know what these birds are like.'

Twitchett was positively beaming. He leaned forward in his chair. 'Time I came clean, I suppose' he said. 'Sorry to disappoint you chaps, but I knew about it all the time. In fact, I must have seen it before any of you.'

Twitchett's claim was greeted with consternation; Listman went very pale. 'Come off it' he said. 'I don't believe a word of it. You've been up in town all day. What's that suit you're wearing?'

'Quite right' said Twitchett. 'But I decided to leave a bit early so that I could take a quick stroll over the marsh. Get a bit of fresh air and see if anything interesting was around.'

'And was there? sneered Listman.

'Not to begin with, I suppose. A few Wheatears, a drake Garganey, a Marsh Warbler and a Jack Snipe were the only interesting birds.'

'Hmmm!' grunted Listman, who had a rather wild look in his eyes.

'I was just leaving when I disturbed it and at the time it didn't seem to make sense; but now of course' he paused as if to emphasise his point 'it all fits. As I came round the corner by the hide, I noticed it sitting on the fence. It was only a silhouette against the rising sun and my first impression was that it was a magpie. Before I could raise my binoculars, though, it dropped off the fence and disappeared below the bank. I didn't see it again. It just seemed to vanish into thin air.'

'What a surprise' muttered Stickler, under his breath but loud enough to bring a scowl to Twitchett's face.

'You saw the blackish cap though?' asked Listman.

'Of course... ' began Twitchett. But suddenly he seemed to be having trouble with his pipe. For a moment or two he tamped it vigourously, brows furrowed in concentration. Finally, his pipe was drawing again. 'Of course not' he said firmly. 'It was definitely grey.'

He looked at Listman suspiciously. 'I thought you were

supposed to have discovered the thing' he said, 'I'm surprised you should make a mistake like that.'

'White along the tail, did you say?' asked Stickler, pressing home the attack.

'Er... Oh yes... er... definitely' said Twitchett, who seemed to be having trouble with his pipe again. He seemed relieved to see the look of real anguish that flitted across Listman's face.

'Immature, of course' said Listman, with the air of one making a last desperate throw.

'Don't be ridiculous, it was clearly an adult.' Twitchett leaned back in his chair with the air of one who has just passed a difficult test. 'Don't worry Listman. I know that you'll be getting the credit on the box over there... ' he nodded towards the television set, which Rossie was just beginning to tune up '... I won't give you away. I've had enough firsts on the marsh. I don't mind giving you this one. Now, let me get you a drink.' He reached for his wallet, and then froze. A shadow flitted across his face and he glanced quickly towards the corner of the bar, where young Bob 'Spottit' was obviously counting up his savings from his odd-jobbery. 'Ah! I forgot. I'll have to see if Rossie can cash me a cheque.'

He walked triumphantly towards the bar. Listman was looking as though he had lost all interest in living and even Stringwell and Stickler were exchanging dark and angry glances. Twitchett was unperturbed. He put their glasses in front of them. 'Now let's see what old "Mr Countryside" makes of us' he said, and settled into his chair.

The broadcast was a great success. Listman had completely recovered by the end of it and Stickler, surprisingly, seemed quite content to be represented by a woolly hat – he didn't after all know where the camera's frame began and ended. 'Mr Countryside' weaved off into the night, supported by his young production assistant, to a rousing cheer from the crowded bar. Even Bob 'Spottit' seemed immensely pleased, although he seemed to have spent more time counting his savings than watching the programme. And they certainly must have been substantial. Two days later he appeared on the marsh with a brand new and very expensive pair of binoculars.

Questions: *1. What was the bird that caused so much fuss? 2. The brown jersey, blue cagoul and grey windcheater were all discussing one particular feature. What was it? 3. Which one species did Twitchett definitely not see during his early morning stroll on the marsh?*

General Knowledge British Isles

All questions refer to British birds.

1. If you saw Lancelot at Slimbridge, what would you have seen?

2. What bird was thought to spend the winter at the bottom of muddy pools?

3. What famous architect had a bird's name?

4. What famous nurse had a bird's name?

5. What two birds advertised 'Guinness is Good for You'?

6. What bird's name also means a flag?

7. What bird's name is a mathematical shape and a toy?

8. What is a remex?

9. What is a rectrix?

10. What is a corvid?

11. Where is the alula?

12. What is egg-shell made from?

13. Woodpeckers are zygodactylous. What does this mean?

14. What was the first bird to appear on a British postage stamp?

15. What two birds appeared on the 4½d National Nature Week stamps in 1963?

16. What do the initials R.S.P.B. stand for?

17. How many feathers are there in a Long-tailed Tit's nest; 500, 1,000, 2,000?

18. What do the initials Y.O.C. stand for?

19. What bird used to appear on the back of a farthing?

20. What is distinctive about a Coot's feet?

21. What British bird has a bridled form?

22. What is a hirundine?

23. What wader has distinctive black 'wing-pits' in winter?

24. What bird sounds like a foghorn?

25. What began at Didsbury in 1889?

26. What bird is commonest in pub and inn names?

27. Who introduced pheasants to Britain?

28. What constellation with a bird's name appears as a cross?

29. What is a murre known as in Britain?

30. What is a dovekie known as in Britain?

31. In late summer, in England, a black parent bird feeds its buff young on a rooftop. What is the species?

32. What two birds are associated with peace and war?

33. What is an aigrette?

34. What bird is linked with the Prince of Wales?

35. What British bird is the Kookaburra related to?

36. What is bird-lime?

37. What on a gull are the mirrors?

38. What common British bird has sub-species on Shetland and St Kilda?

39. What British bird was Pinguinus impennis?

40. What British bird has a hepatic phase?

41. What do the initials B.T.O. stand for?

42. What is unusual about the feet of gannets, cormorants and pelicans?

43. What do the initials S.O.C. stand for?

44. What is the nail on a duck or goose?

45. What British bird is named after a bird artist?

46. Name three British birds which begin 'Long-tailed'.

47. Name three British birds which begin 'Red-breasted'.

48. What is the Barred Woodpecker now called?

49. What is a tystie?

50. Name five breeding birds whose names contain other birds' names.

51. Name four British birds whose names contain the name of a marine animal.

52. What is a bird's maxilla?

53. What is a 'comic' tern?

54. What four birds appeared on the 1966 'British Birds' stamps?

55. What is the Scarlet Grosbeak now called?

56. What are known as Horned Larks in America?

57. What bird's call is known as 'sharming'?

58. What bird's call is known as 'bleating'?

59. What is distinctive about a juvenile Goldcrest?

60. What is unusual about a recently hatched Crossbill?

61. What four British bird's names begin 'Grey'?

62. Which bird bred in Britain in 1985 for the first time in 70 years?

63. Which four birds appeared on the 1980 stamps that commemorated the centenary of the Wild Bird Protection Act?

64. What do the initials B.O.U. stand for?

SO YOU THINK YOU'RE A TWITCHER.

From time to time, we read in the press that hundreds of scruffy individuals have, for no reason at first obvious, descended *en masse* on an unsuspecting part of Britain. The explanation generally turns out to be that a RARE BIRD has turned up. As likely as not, it is an undistinguished and bedraggled greyish-brown sparrow-sized bird, skulking in some inhospitable bush or damp swamp, scared almost out of its follicles by the relentless pursuit of these over-excited chaps. Let us look at them more closely.

At the top of the league are the MANIACS. Normally unemployed and unemployable, they spend their every waking moment following up rarities: they communicate via the *grapevine*, administered from a number of mysterious telephone numbers scattered in a network across the British Isles; they will travel around the country, regardless of distance, often driving through the night, so as not to miss a thing. They never carry field guides.

There aren't all that many maniacs. More numerous is the conventional TWITCHER. The twitcher may well have a job, in which case he is faced each time with an agonising choice when a rarity turns up: does he take time off work on some pretext, or does he wait for the weekend and hope that the bird is still there. His decision will depend on time, distance and species. However, if he chooses the former too often, he will soon graduate to maniac. He may carry a field guide, but it will be to a foreign avifauna, to which the putative rarity belongs.

After twitchers come BIRDERS. They are more relaxed. It is unlikely that they would take time off work to pursue a rarity, unless it was a matter of taking a long lunch-hour or knocking off a bit early. But their weekends and holidays will be spent 'birding', and they will then tap into the grapevine on a regional, but probably not national, scale. They might have a field guide in the car.

By far the largest class has no official name. We will merely call them BIRD-WATCHERS. They take their hobby quite seriously, but it is not necessarily the most important thing in their lives. They cannot therefore be birders; but they are clearly superior to dudes (see below), because they can identify pretty well all the familiar British species, and probably have the skill to work out the others from descriptions, and by using the field guides that they nearly always carry.

At the very bottom of the hierarchy is the DUDE. He is a normal and well-adjusted person; but he's not very good at identifying birds. He may not even be good enough to carry a field guide, but he will certainly refer to the wall-charts pinned up in the nearest hide.

Which are you? After reading this preamble, you've probably got a pretty good idea already. But the class boundaries are not always clear-cut; so answer these questions and be sure!

1. You are best man at your brother's wedding in Yorkshire. On the evening before you receive a phone call about a White-rumped Swift seen going to roost at Portland Bill. Do you:

   a) Persuade your brother that she's not worth it and that he should call it all off?
   b) Ring the vicar and ask him to pray that it stays for a couple of days?
   c) Philosophically decide that the wedding is more important and that there is bound to be another White-rumped Swift some day?
   d) Move the reception to 'The Devenish Arms' at Portland?

2. It is your wife's birthday. You have managed to save just enough money to buy her the the present she wants when you are offered a place on a plane to Fair Isle to see a Cretzschmar's Bunting and a Bimaculated Lark. Do you:

   a) Tell your wife it is out of stock but will be arriving next week and pray that the pools come up?
   b) Ring up your not-so-friendly bank manager and persuade him that a large life-list is really a long-term investment?
   c) Invent a distant Scottish branch of the family and claim that a relative has died?
   d) Decide that buntings and larks are all one-day birds and wouldn't wait for you to arrive anyway?

111

3. *It is your birthday and a group of friends have arranged a party and have fed you copious amounts of alcohol. As a final present, the phone rings with news of a Spoon-billed Sandpiper at Cley. You are carried out to the car and driven up to see it. All of you see the bird and after a few drinks to celebrate you pass out. The following day the bird has gone and you find that you can't remember anything about the previous 24 hours. Do you:*

a) *Tick it off and hope that none of your friends ask any questions?*

b) *Decide that as you don't remember it it can't be counted?*

c) *Borrow a friend's notebook and copy out his description just in case?*

d) *Decide that a few drinks might help you to remember?*

4. *It is your first trip to the Scilly Isles and one lunchtime you suddenly see people running towards Hugh Town. Do you:*

a) *Start running there yourself and hope you will meet someone who can tell you what's happening?*

b) *Decide that they are all trying to get to the 'Bishop and Wolf' before it shuts?*

c) *Hijack a bicycle from a passing local and head for town?*

d) *Carry on walking to look for the Common Rosefinch that was seen at Watermill?*

5. *You are sitting in a hide at Minsmere looking for a Western Sandpiper. The birder next to you, who is a rather large and belligerent type, suddenly announces he has seen it. You realise that the bird he has seen is only a Dunlin. Do you:*

a) *Ask him where it is in relation to the Dunlin?*

b) *Keep quiet and continue looking, hoping that someone else will say something?*

c) *Tell him that he should go back to his 'Observer's Book' and start again?*

d) *Diplomatically give him a let-out by saying 'Isn't that the aberrant Dunlin that's here as well?'*

6. *While on the Scilly Isles a Veery is found in a small field which is surrounded by a tall, thick hedge. There is only one vantage point by a gate and there are four hundred people there all trying to see it and you are at the back. Do you:*

a) *Decide to go away and return when everyone has seen it?*

b) *Shout 'Eskimo Curlew at Porthloo' and hope that they will all rush off to see that?*

c) *Use your telescope to beat your way to the front?*

d) *Climb into the next door field and try to peer through the hedge?*

7.   *You have just left Fair Isle one autumn having seen many new birds. On getting back home you receive a phone call to tell you that one of the two Richard's Pipits that were there has been trapped and is in fact a Blyth's Pipit. Not knowing which of the two it was, do you:*

a) *Immediately arrange to fly back up there.*

b) *Decide that as you saw both birds you can count it.*

c) *Decide that as you don't know which it was, you can't count it.*

d) *Say that you thought it was a Blyth's Pipit all along but didn't like to say so.*

Your Score.

1. a) A difficult solution to achieve, which may depend on whether you can get a refund on your present. *3 points.*

b) A harmless but probably ineffective action. *2 points.*

c) A defeatist attitude, not worthy of a dedicated twitcher. *1 point.*

d) If possible, this would be the best solution, providing plenty of scope for celebrating once it's on your list. *4 points.*

2   a) Praying often forms part of a twitcher's lifestyle, but never for miracles. *3 points.*

b) Not recommended unless your bank manager is also a twitcher, in which case he may still say no and pinch the place for himself. *2 points.*

c) A good ploy, to be used in emergencies only, as you will soon run out of relatives. *4 points.*

d) Too defeatist, even if it is true. Always go for it! *1 point.*

3   a) Always tick it off, after all, there were witnesses. *4 points*.

     b) This is an honest but stupid way of thinking. *1 point*.

     c) No need for this level of subterfuge: a simple tick will do. *2 points*.

     d) They might also make you forget what you've forgotten. *3 points*.

4   a) Definitely the best move. If in doubt, run. *4 points*.

     b) A sound possibility, but the likelihood of error should make you reject it. *1 point*. unless you would have run to the pub in any case, in which case *4 points*.

     c) This has merit and extra speed, but will not endear you to the islanders. *3 points*.

     d) An understandable choice if you need it but there is no guarantee that it will be there and, anyway, they are not very interesting. *2 points*.

5   a) A classic line, guaranteed to cause amusement and, possibly, a broken nose. *3 points*.

     b) Keeping a low profile is all part of good birding, but do you really want to get away with it? *2 points*

     c) Said firmly and with conviction, this might work. Make sure that you are a BUPA member. *1 point*.

     d) A nice reply. He saves face, and you save yours. *4 points*.

6   a) While this often works and prevents conflict, it is not recommended for the serious twitcher. *2 points*.

     b) You have to choose your bird and its location very carefully. Learn how to throw your voice. *3 points*.

     c) Rather extreme. It can throw prisms out of alignment and blood is not easily cleaned off lenses. *1 point*.

     d) Discreetly done, this offers the best hope, although the local landowner may not take kindly to it. *4 points*.

7   a) If you've got the time and the cash, go for it! *3 points*.

     b) An eminently sound piece of logic. *4 points*.

     c) Very honest, but it won't help you to get your list into the four hundreds. *1 point*.

     d) This approach doesn't really help your field creditability unless you can back it up. *2 points*.

For an analysis of your score, turn to page 127.

Answers

Page 12

1. From the description given, the bird might have been a young Barred Warbler but, as Twitchett mentions seeing a late Fieldfare, the bird must have been seen in spring when it would have had a pale eye and would have shown barring. **2.** Green Woodpecker. Golden Orioles are rarely seen away from trees and seldom on the ground. Green Woodpeckers often feed on the ground for ants, and show a lot of green and yellow when they fly off. **3.** Female Cuckoos are not brown. The two races of Bluethroat are indistinguishable as females. **4.** Dotterel.

Page 13

1. Road Runners. **2.** 25,000. **3.** Garden Warbler; it doesn't use a nest box. **4.** Immediately in front of the eyes. **5.** *The Magic Flute* by Mozart. **6.** Swift. **7.** 'Goldie', the Golden Eagle. **8.** Reeve. **9.** They are all sub-species. **10.** It breeds on stony ground and has a call like a curlew. **11.** Grest Crested Grebe. **12.** Pen. **13.** Twenty-four. **14.** A rookery. **15.** Tawny Owl; there are none in Ireland. **16.** Quail; its call sounds like "whet-my-lips". **17.** The National Audubon Society. **18.** Goldfinch.

Page 14

19. Garden; all the others can be the first name of a warbler *and* another species. **20.** Blackbird, Chaffinch or Wren, all of which can achieve populations of 10-15 million birds. **21.** Bempton Cliffs, Humberside. **22.** Greyhen. **23.** Merlin. **24.** Dartford Warbler; it is the only one that is resident. **25.** Off the coast of Brazil. **26.** Yellowhammer. **27.** A herd. **28.** Divers. **29.** Albatross. **30.** Gannet. **31.** Rhea. **32.** Gilbert White. **33.** Skua; it cannot have the prefix 'Common'. **34.** Ducks of the merganser tribe. **35.** Osprey. **36.** Starling. **37.** Alcatraz, the island prison off the coast of California. **38.** Bass Rock; the specific name of the Gannet is *bassana*. **39.** Collared Dove. **40.** Turnstone; it has never bred in Britain. **41.** The last Passenger Pigeon.

Page 15

42. Meadow Pipit. **43.** Ravens. **44.** The male has a red nape, the female doesn't. **45.** Canaries; they were used to detect the presence of poisonous gas. **46.** Fulmar. **47.** Green. **48.** Heron; 'Frank'; is also a country name for it. **49.** Skokholm. **50.** Members of the gannet family. **51.** Hawfinch. **52.** Great Skua. **53.** Wisp. **54.** Barn Owl. **55.** Avocet. **56.** Swallow. **57.** Swift. **58.** An owl, in Edward Lear's rhyme 'The Owl and the Pussycat'. **59.** The Bearded Tit is not a member of the true tit family; it is closely related to the babblers. **60.** The Goshawk. **61.** A diurnal bird of prey, i.e. eagles, hawks and falcons, but not owls. **62.** The continental race has a black belly; the British race has a chestnut belly. **63.** Kestrel. **64.** An owl, in Grey's *Elegy Written in a Country Churchyard*.

Page 17

1. Swallow; in winter it is not in Britain but in Africa. **2.** Snow Goose and Bar-headed Goose; they are not found genuinely wild in Britain. (Snow Goose might conceivably be, but not in Buckinghamshire). **3.** The 'Barn Owl' claimed by Twitchett was actually a Short-eared Owl; even without his sketch, we wouldn't believe he'd seen a Barn Owl at that time of the day. The 'Buzzard' was in fact a Sparrowhawk.

Page 24

1. Ruby-throated Humming Bird, found in the eastern United States. **2.** California Condor. **3.** Prairie Falcon. **4.** Elegant Trogon; Eustace was plainly unaware that they don't lay their eggs on the ground.

Page 25

1. By plastering mud round the edge of the hole. **2.** They have a nasal salt gland for excreting the salt. **3.** A form of feather maintenance involving rubbing ants into the feathers to exploit their formic acid. **4.** One bird of a pair preening the other. **5.** Birds of Prey. **6.** To distract a predator away from its nest or young. **7.** The sudden change in direction or banking of wildfowl as they land. **8.** It is active at dusk or dawn. **9.** By taking a beakful of water and lifting their heads to swallow. **10.** By dipping their bill in the water and drinking continuously. **11.** Displaying aggression with wings raised and head laid back. **12.** Nightjar. **13.** A bird that spends all its time at sea, apart from breeding. **14.** An irregular migration associated with changing food supplies. **15.** Owls. **16.** Arctic Skua; it steals food from terns and gulls. **17.** By dipping their beaks into the surface of the water in flight. **18.** By soaking their breast feathers in it.

Page 26

19. Fulmar. **20.** Poorwill (an American Nightjar). **21.** Sonar. **22.** Young Greylag Geese, during Lorenz's studies of imprinting. **23.** One that eats cereal and grain. **24.** One that eats grass. **25.** One whose young leave the nest straight after hatching. **26.** One whose young remain in the nest for some time after hatching. **27.** Swift. **28.** Snipe. **29.** Rook. **30.** Honey Buzzard. **31.** Wigeon. **32.** Dipper. **33.** Roding. **34.** Black Grouse (male). **35.** It acts as a stimulus for the young to peck at the parent bird's bill, thus triggering the release of food. **36.** Egyptian Vulture. **37.** Song Thrush. **38.** A decorated 'garden' outside the nest used to attract a female. **39.** It uses a thorn to poke grubs out of wood. **40.** Dunnock, Meadow Pipit, Reed Warbler. **41.** A fruit-eater.

Page 27

42. Flamingos. **43.** A collective and noisy demonstration against a predator. **44.** To stir up food. **45.** A fish-eater. **46.** The laying of eggs in another bird's nest; e.g. the Cuckoo. **47.** Shrikes or butcher birds. **48.** Descending from a height by a falcon or other bird of prey onto its victim. **49.** By ejecting the eggs or young of the host bird. **50.** Opening a milk bottle. **51.** Phalaropes. **52.** Because it feeds its young on migrating birds, which are most plentiful in autumn. **53.** Hobby. **54.** Under their feet. **55.** Penguins. **56.** Oven-birds. **57.** They obtain their food from the backs of large mammals. **58.** A sudden panic flight in a colony for no clear reason. **59.** It is another word for moult. **60.** Because they pick up the lead shot used by anglers instead of grit. **61.** A communal display ground. **62.** Feed on peanuts in bird-feeders. **63.** The feral birds don't migrate. **64.** The male takes care of the eggs and young.

Page 29

1. Whimbrel, which is a summer visitor. **2.** The female Merlin was a Kestrel. The Redstart must have been a Black Redstart. The Short-eared Owl was a Long-eared Owl; the Short-eared does *not* roost in bushes. The Black-necked Grebe was a Slavonian Grebe.

Page 33

1. Violet-green Swallow. It occurs in the western United States. **2.** Twitchett's description is not convincing; the bird could have been a Kestrel. Female Red-footed Falcons have a distinctive head pattern. **3.** As the Purple Heron was his 'best' bird, Twitchett can't have seen any very rare plovers. The seven must therefore have been: Lapwing, Dotterel, Grey Plover, Golden Plover, Ringed Plover, Little Ringed Plover and Kentish Plover.

Page 34

1. Ostrich, Emu, Cassowary, Rhea. **2.** Those to the west migrate over Gibraltar, those to the east over the Bosphorus. **3.** Honeyguides. **4.** Larks. **5.** Tits. **6.** International Council for Bird Preservation. **7.** Willow Warbler. **8.** The Roc. **9.** New Guinea and Australia. **10.** Mauritius. **11.** Hummingbirds. **12.** Seabird droppings, in particular from cormorants in South America. **13.** Konrad Lorenz. **14.** A main migration route. **15.** An American woodpecker. **16.** A wader. **17.** Hummingbirds. **18.** The Canary Islands and Madeira.

Page 35

19. 56-76. (The actual figure is 66). **20.** The Emus, after Australian artillery had failed to drive an invasion of 20,000 birds from Western Australia. **21.** Hawaii. **22.** Australia: it is a member of the butcher-bird family. **23.** Skuas. **24.** Banding. **25.** South America. **26.** A dodo. **27.** Harrier-hawk. **28.** Resplendent Quetzal or Resplendent Trogon. **29.** Cock. **30.** Bald Eagle. **31.** Black Swan. **32.** The nests of Edible-nest Swiftlets. **33.** The oldest known fossil bird. **34.** Flightless running birds; i.e. Ostrich, emus, rheas, cassowaries and kiwis. **35.** A stork. **36.** Shoebill. **37.** 9,000. **38.** Galapagos. **39.** Hummingbirds (330 species). **40.** 100,000 million. **41.** John James Audubon. **42.** From the plumes on its head, which resemble quill pens.

Page 36

43. Emperor Penguin; it only touches ice or water. **44.** A tern. **45.** A shearwater. **46.** Their ranges overlap. **47.** Partially webbed. **48.** 1662. **49.** China and Japan. **50.** North America. **51.** An eagle is reputed to have dropped a tortoise on his head. **52.** The Eagle (in the City Road, in the original version of 'Pop Goes the Weasel'). **53.** Azure-winged Magpie. **54.** Crested Coot. **55.** Hawaii (68 species). **56.** House Sparrow. **57.** Cuckoos. **58.** Pheasants, quails and Partridges. **59.** Ostrich. **60.** Swifts. **61.** Megapodes or Mallee Fowl. **62.** Carmine Bee-eaters from the backs of bustards. **63.** They are both extinct. **64.** Its tail is shaped like a lyre.

Page 41

1. St Ives in Cornwall, close to the Scillies and even nearer to the Hayle estuary where American waders often turn up. **2.** A House Martin, which has a white rump. Perspective and size are always problems when sea-watching. **3.** Sabine's Gull; Long-tailed Skua; Great Shearwater.

Page 43

1. The Goosander was almost certainly a Red-breasted Merganser. The Pink-footed Goose was a Greylag Goose. The Spotted Flycatcher does not arrive in Britain until June. 2. Avocet.

Page 44

1. Knot (*Calidris canutus*). 2. Goldfinch. 3. Chiffchaff. 4. Lapwing ('peewit'). 5. Treecreeper. 6. Reed Bunting. 7. Long-tailed Duck. 8. House Martin 9. Bearded Tit. 10. Long-tailed Duck or Pintail. 11. Red Kite. 12. Redstart. 13. Hooded Crow. 14. Mistle Thrush. 15. Storm Petrel. 16. Eider Duck. 17. Moorhen. 18. Sand Martin. 19. Osprey. 20. Honey Buzzard.

Page 45

21. Starling. 22. Magpie. 23. Bittern. 24. Redshank. 25. Nuthatch. 26. Fieldfare. 27. Blackcap. 28. Garden Warbler. 29. House Sparrow. 30. Song Thrush. 31. Spoonbill. 32. Puffin (or Razorbill). 33. Curlew, Kittiwake, Cuckoo, Chiffchaff, Chough, Jackdaw or Hoopoe. 34. Shearwaters, Lapwing, Swift. 35. Bullfinch. 36. Blue or Great Tit. 37. Wigeon. 38. Redshank. 39. Nightjar. 40. Corncrake. 41. Green Woodpecker (or parrot). 42. Kingfisher. 43. Red Grouse. 44. Meadow Pipit or Twite. 45. Bee-eater, Kingfisher, Oystercatcher. Honey Buzzard, Bean Goose, Goshawk, Sparrowhawk.

Page 46

46. Nuthatch, Nutcracker, Flycatchers, Mistle Thrush, Carrion Crow, Chaffinch, Hawfinch. 47. Stone-curlew. 48. Short-eared Owl. 49. Dunnock. 50. Robin. 51. Shelduck. 52. Coal Tit. 53. Montagu's Harrier, Lady Amherst's Pheasant, Cetti's Warbler, Savi's Warbler, Leach's Petrel. 54. Manx Shearwater, Kentish Plover, Dartford Warbler, Sandwich Tern. 55. Avocet. 56. Shoveler. 57. Great Tit. 58. Grasshopper Warbler. 59. Blackbird. 60. Dipper. 61. Moorhen. 62. Rook. 63. Little Grebe. 64. Long-tailed Tit.

Page 51

1. The Black-headed Gull; it doesn't breed on cliff ledges. 2. Storm Petrel and Manx Shearwater; they only fly up to their burrows at night. 3. It was the *Titanic*.

Page 52

1. Crossbill. 2. Robin. 3. Delius 4. 'A Robin redbreast in a cage'. 5. Aristophanes. 6. Daphne du Maurier. 7. Duck. 8. Homer. 9. Horus. 10. Vaughan Williams. 11. Cuckoo. 12. Song Thrush 13. Blackbird. 14. The Pigeon.

Page 53

15. Robin. 16. Chiffchaff. 17. Blackcap. 18. The Jackdaw in 'The Jackdaw of Rheims'. 19. Pelican. 20. Cuckoo. 'In June, he changes his tune'. 21. Swan. 22. Robin. 23. Quail, Cuckoo and Nightingale. 24. *Alouette, gentille alouette*. 25. Owl. 26. Swan. 27. Coot Club. 28. Snipe. 29. Sparrow. 30. Stravinsky. 31. Tennyson, of the eagle. 32. The Raven, Edgar Allen Poe. 33. Hans Christian Anderson. 34. 'The common Cormorant or Shag'. 35. Keats.

Page 54

36. Flamingo. 37. Shelley, in an ode to the Skylark. 38. Kookaburra. 39. The Heron. It was served to Edward III as a symbol of cowardice by Robert of Artois. 40. A handsaw or heron. 41. Skylark. 42. Crane. 43. Schubert. 44. Swift. 45. Long John Silver's parrot. 46. Cormorant. 47. Phoenix. 48. Green Woodpecker. 49. 'The Hen' 50. Stravinsky. 51. Sir Arthur Sullivan. 52. Coot and hern (Heron). 53. Lewis Carroll. 54. Thomas Love Peacock. 55. Mockingbird.

Page 55

56. Quails, in Exodus. 57. Rimsky Korsakov. 58. Rossini. 59. Polynesia. 60. Wren. 61. Geese. 62. White Stork. 63. Owl. 64. Shakespeare, in *The Merry Wives of Windsor*.

Page 57

1. The female Garganey was, in fact, a Blue-winged Teal, which has blue wing patches. 2. The female Scaup was a Tufted Duck, which can show a white patch around the bill. The Black-throated Diver was a Red-throated Diver, which can be quite dark above, but has a characteristic up-turned bill. The Little Gull was an immature Kittiwake, which has a white crown and uniform back and wing coverts. 3. The Chukar, which is an introduced gamebird.

Page 63

1. The Lesser-spotted Woodpecker. They don't occur that far north. 2. Islay; the only place where all three species occur together. 3. Red-throated Divers.

Page 68

1. Mute Swan (up to more than 40 lb.) 2. Goldcrest (one-sixth of an ounce) 3. Manx Shearwater; just under 30 years old. 4. Lady Amherst's Pheasant. 5. Garden Warbler. 6. Raven. 7. Skylark. 8. Wren. 9. Swallow. 10. Hawfinch. 11. Eider. 12. Lapwing. 13. Kestrel. 14. Blue Tit. 15. Razorbill; over 450 ft. 16. Velvet Scoter; 3 minutes. 17. House Sparrow, Blackbird or Feral Pigeon; all may have 5. 18. Starling (over one million). 19. Goldcrest.

Page 69

20. Blackbird; 17 young from 4 broods. **21.** Bittern. **22.** Fulmar. **23.** Blackcap; 10-12 days. **24.** Male Swift. **25.** Avocet. **26.** Swift. **27.** Grey Heron. (Curlew would be if straightened out.) **28.** Snipe. **29.** Blue Tit, Robin, Blackbird or Song Thrush. **30.** Gannet. **31.** Dotterel; recorded at 4,265 ft. **32.** Wren. **33.** Sparrowhawk. (The female can be nearly twice as heavy as the male.) **34.** Woodcock. **35.** Swift. **36.** Chiffchaff. **37.** Osprey (one species). The Hoopoe would also be a correct answer but it doesn't breed regularly in Britain. **38.** Ostrich (345 lb.) **39.** Bee hummingbird (one-eighteenth of an ounce). **40.** Manx Shearwater, from Wales to South Australia.

Page 70

41. Red-billed Quelea (Africa). **42.** Wilson's Storm Petrel. **43.** Andean Condor. **44.** Arctic Tern (Arctic-Antarctic). **45.** Wandering Albatross (11 ft 6 in.) **46.** Australian Pelican. **47.** Royal Albatross (c. 80 days). **48.** Grey Partridge (c. 19). **49.** Spine-tailed Swift. **50.** Kori Bustard. **51.** Alpine Chough. **52.** Ruppell's Griffon Vulture; 37,000 ft. **53.** Elf Owl (U.S.A.) **54.** Mallee Fowl (Australia). **55.** Sociable Weaver (up to 300, Africa). **56.** Owls. **57.** Amethystine Hummingbird (80 beats per second). **58.** Antarctic Skua. **59.** Reeve's Pheasant; over 8 ft. **60.** Falcons. **61.** Colombia (over 1,700). **62.** Tyrant Flycatchers (over 360 species in North and South America). **63.** Albatrosses. **64.** Penguins.

Page 75

1. Barn Owl or Moorhen. **2.** The mast of a ship. **3.** Woodchat Shrike. **4.** Eleonora's Falcon.

Page 76

1. Mandarin, Wood Duck, Ruddy Duck, Egyptian Goose. **2.** Lady Amherst's Pheasant, Ring-necked Parakeet. **3.** Marsh Harrier, Honey Buzzard. **4.** Ruff, Avocet, Stone-curlew, Black-tailed Godwit. **5.** Cetti's, Savi's, Dartford and Marsh Warblers. **6.** Golden Oriole, Bearded Tit, Black Redstart, Firecrest, Red-backed Shrike, Cirl Bunting. **7.** Crested Tit, Scottish Crossbill, Snow Bunting. **8.** Capercaillie, Ptarmigan. **9.** Whimbrel, Greenshank, Red-necked Phalarope. **10.** Skuas (Arctic and Great)**11.** Black-throated Diver, Slavonian Grebe, Leach's Petrel, Osprey. **12.** Black Guillemot. **13.** Slavonian Grebe. **14.** White-fronted Goose, Brent Goose. **15.** Little Owl. **16.** Grasshopper Warbler, Sedge Warbler, Blackcap, Garden Warbler, Whitethroat, Willow Warbler, Chiffchaff, Wood Warbler.

Page 77

17. Smew. 18. Marsh Tit. 19. Ring-necked Parakeet. 20. Ortolan. 21. Mediterranean Gull. 22. Red-necked Phalarope, Whimbrel, Leach's Petrel. 23. None. 24. Stonechat. 25. West Germany. 26. Norway. 27. Britain. 28. Greece. 29. Spain. 30. Iceland. 31. Portugal. 32. Switzerland, Luxembourg. 33. Iceland, Ireland.

Page 78

34. Finland. 35. Norway. 36. Greece. 37. Rumania. 38. Greece. 39. None. 40. Spain. 41. Iceland. 42. Portugal. 43. Spain. 44. Italy. 45. None. 46. Rock Partridge, Corsican Nuthatch, Scottish Crossbill, Citril Finch. 47. Portugal and Greece. 48. Holland. 49. Southern Sweden (a few miles closer than Iceland). 50. Norway. 51. Norway.

Page 79

52. Portugal. 53. Slavonian Grebe. 54. Holland. 55. Fulmar. 56. Greylag Goose, Canada Goose. 57. Egyptian Vulture, Lammergeier, Black Vulture, Griffon Vulture. 58. Eleonora's Falcon. 59. None. 60. Cyprus Warbler. 61. Blackcap. 62. Redwing. 63. Redpoll. 64. Mallard, Water Rail, Pied Wagtail, Wheatear, Wren. (Lapwing, Swallow and Collared Dove breed *irregularly* in Iceland.)

Page 83

1. A Chough. 2. Because all of the North American gulls with black heads have been seen in Britain. 3. Red-legged Kittiwake.

Page 84

1. Lapwing. 2. Nuthatch. 3. Wryneck. 4. Red-legged Partridge. 5. Sanderling. 6. Kittiwake. 7. Dunnock. 8. Chough. 9. Long-tailed Duck. 10. Garganey. 11. Goldfinch. 12. Corn Bunting. 13. Short-eared Owl. 14. Snipe. 15. Willow Tit.

Page 85

16. Dipper. 17. Oystercatcher. 18. Stone Curlew. 19. House Martin. 20. Rock Dove. 21. Crested Tit. 22. Penduline Tit. 23. Rock Pipit. 24. Shore Lark. 25. Two-barred Crossbill. 26. Snow Bunting. 27. Greenfinch, Siskin, Golden Oriole. 28. Moorhen. 29. Treecreeper, Chough. 30. Sandwich Tern. 31. Coot. 32. Puffin. 33. Starling. All the others nest in colonies. 34. Dunnock. All the others are named after their songs. 35. Arctic Tern. All the others dive for their food from the surface.

36. Reed Warbler. All the others occur in Britain in winter. **37.** Yellowhammer. All the others have white rumps. **38.** Shelduck. All the others nest in holes in trees. **39.** Chaffinch. All the others have black crowns. **40.** Black-headed Gull. All the others have forked tails. **41.** Coot. All the others have yellow eyes; the Coot has a red one. **42.** Fulmar. All the others breed solely on islands. **43.** Sandpiper. All the others can be prefixed with 'Little'. **44.** Shoveler. All the others have male birds with knobs on their bills. **45.** Yellow Wagtail. All the others are regular hosts to the cuckoo's brood parasitism. **46.** Long-tailed Tit. All the others use nestboxes. **47.** Common Gull. All the others have red spots on their bills in breeding plumage. **48.** Raven. All the others have red legs in the breeding season. **49.** Song Thrush. Its eggs are spotted; all the others are plain blue. **50.** Woodchat. It is a shrike; all the others are chats. **51.** Nutcracker. All the others have bred in Britain. **52.** Capercaillie. All the others occur naturally; the Capercaillie was introduced after it became extinct. (Ptarmigan would be an acceptable alternative answer; it is the only one with summer and winter plumages, and feathered feet.) **53.** Bombay Duck. It isn't a duck, it's a fish. **54.** Kestrel. All the others can have another bird's name as a prefix; Thrush Nightingale, Curlew Sandpiper and Hawk Owl. **55.** Blue Tit. All the others have summer and winter plumages. **56.** Garden Warbler. All the others have black throats on the males in the breeding season.

Page 87

57. Great Spotted Woodpecker. All the others have display flights. **58.** Snow Bunting. All the others breed in England. **59.** Snipe. All the others can be prefixed by a colour. **60.** Great Crested Grebe. All the others have down-curved bills. **61.** Skylark. All the others have breast bands. **62.** Sand Martin. All the others nest on the ground. **63.** Coot. All the others have yellow bills. **64.** Osprey. All the others catch fish with their bills; Ospreys use their talons.

Page 91

1. 107. **2.** Green Woodpeckers don't drum and Great Snipe don't breed in Denmark. **3.** Great Snipe are very rare in May. It was more likely to have been a common Snipe or a Woodcock.

Page 92

1. Passenger Pigeon. **2.** A sheathbill. **3.** Eagle. **4.** Kestrel. **5.** Black Redstart. **6.** Ducks. **7.** Their food, in particular crustaceans such as shrimps. **8.** The Isle of May. **9.** 9,500. **10.** Night Heron. **11.** Fulmar. **12.** Swallow. **13.** Peacock. **14.** Norwich. **15.** An American bird of prey. **16.** Bullfinch, Brambling, Arctic Redpoll, Goldfinch.

Page 93

17. White Stork. 18. Little Tern. 19. St Louis. 20. Golden Pheasant. 21. Cuba. 22. Central and South America. 23. Sheffield Wednesday. 24. Pigeons. 25. Heligoland. 26. Australian Crane. 27. Cuckoo. 28. Skimmer. 29. Mallard. 30. An American wading bird. 31. Peacock. 32. Alaska. 33. Baltimore. 34. Little Bittern. 35. The Wryneck (*Jynx torquilla*). In the past, it was used as a charm to defeat an enemy or ensure the return of a loved one. 36. A South American stork. 37. An African stork.

Page 94

38. Ivory Gull. 39. White-spotted and Red-spotted. 40. 194. 41. 'Two Owls and a Hen, Four Larks and a Wren.' 42. Wren. 43. 14 (White-tailed Eagle not included). 44. Mandarin Duck. 45. Killdeer. 46. Red-tailed Hawk, American Kestrel. 47. 1000. 48. Swansea (Swans) and Cardiff (Bluebirds). 49. Little Gull. 50. There is a Short-toed species of each. 51. Black-browed Albatross. 52. 540. 53. Green Woodpecker. 54. Parrot. *Flaubert's Parrot* was a well-known novel by Julian Barnes. 55. Seagull. 56. There is a dove in the hologram. 57. A cuckoo's nest.

Page 95

58. The Owl, in Edward Lear's rhyme 'The Owl and the Pussycat'. 59. Loch of the Lowes. It is not an R.S.P.B. reserve. 60. Sparrow. A vulture can be Bearded; a tern can be Whiskered; a warbler can be Moustached. 61. White-tailed Eagle. 62. T. Rex. 63. Albatross. 64. Paul Gallico wrote *The Snow Goose*; Peter Scott illustrated the first edition; Jenny Agutter and Richard Harris starred in the film.

Page 97

1. Yellow Wagtails wouldn't have been there; they must have been Blue-headed Wagtails. Treecreepers do not occur in the area; it must have been a Short-toed Treecreeper. 2. The Rook is a scarce winter visitor to the area; it must have been a Carrion Crow. The Lesser Black-backed Gull is only seen in winter and must have been a dark-plumaged Herring Gull. 3. Canada Goose.

Page 98

1. White. 2. Chestnut. 3. Yellow. 4. Pink. 5. Red. 6. Dark brown. 7. Yellow. 8. Red. 9. White. 10. White. 11. Black. 12. White. 13. White. 14. Black. 15. Grey. 16. Chestnut. 17. Blue. 18. White. 19. Brown. 20. Brown.

Page 99

21. Pink. 22. Black. 23. Blue. 24. White. 25. Dark brown. 26. Grey. 27. White. 28. Black and yellow at the base. 29. Off-white. 30. Blue. 31. Red. 32. Brown/chestnut. 33. Black. 34. White. 35. Grey. 36. Red. 37. Green. 38. Pink. 39. Black. 40. Rufous. 41. Yellow. 42. White. 43. Green. 44. Grey. 45. Yellow. 46. Yellow. 47. Yellow.

Page 100

48. Red. 49. White with small red spots. 50. Blue with black specks. 51. Cream. 52. Brown. 53. Grey. 54. Yellow. 55. Green. 56. Chestnut/orange. 57. Pale brown. 58. Red. 59. White. 60. Grey. 61. Yellow. 62. Grey. 63. White. 64. Black with purple sheen.

Page 106

1. Great Spotted Cuckoo. 2. The bird's calls. 3. Marsh Warbler. It doesn't arrive until late May and the events are stated to have taken place in March.

Page 107

1. A Bewick's Swan. 2. Swallow. 3. Sir Christopher Wren. 4. Florence Nightingale. 5. Toucan and Ostrich. 6. Bunting. 7. Kite. 8. A flight feather, from the wing. 9. A tail feather. 10. A member of the crow family. 11. It is a reduced wing-feather, the so-called 'bastard wing'. 12. Calcium carbonate. 13. They have two forward-pointing and two backward-pointing toes on each foot. 14. A dove, on the 3d Victory issue in 1946. 15. Great Spotted Woodpecker and Long-tailed Tit. 16. Royal Society for the Protection of Birds. 17. 2,000.

Page 108

18. Young Ornithologists' Club. 19. Wren. 20. They have lobes of skin along the toes. 21. Guillemot. 22. A swallow or martin. 23. Grey Plover. 24. Bittern. 25. The Royal Society for the Protection of Birds. 26. Swan. 27. The Romans. 28. Cygnus. 29. Guillemot. 30. Little Auk. 31. Starling. 32. Dove and hawk. 33. Plume feather from an egret, used in millinery. 34. Ostrich: three Ostrich feathers form his crest. 35. Kingfisher. 36. A sticky substance (made of holly bark and linseed), used for catching birds. 37. White patches on black wing-tips. 38. Wren. 39. Great Auk. 40. Cuckoo; hepatic refers to the rare rufous-brown or 'liver-coloured' phase. 41. British Trust for Ornithology. 42. They have webs between all four toes.

43. Scottish Ornithologists' Club. **44.** The coloured tip to the upper mandible. **45.** Bewick's Swan. **46.** Duck, Skua, Tit. **47.** Goose, Merganser, Flycatcher. **48.** Lesser Spotted Woodpecker. **49.** Black Guillemot. **50.** Sparrowhawk, Hen Harrier, Woodcock, Stone-curlew, Parrot Crossbill. **51.** Barnacle Goose, Oystercatcher, Herring Gull, Turtle Dove. **52.** Its upper jaw or mandible. **53.** An unidentifiable Common or Arctic Tern. **54.** Black-headed Gull, Blue Tit, Robin, Blackbird. **55.** Common Rosefinch. **56.** Shore Larks. **57.** Water Rail. **58.** Snipe. **59.** It has no crown markings. **60.** Its bill isn't crossed. **61.** Heron, Partridge, Plover. **62.** White-tailed Eagle. **63.** Kingfisher, Moorhen, Dipper, Yellow Wagtail. **64.** British Ornithologists' Union.

So You Think You're A Twitcher
Analysis of your score.

25 points or over. Maniac. See you at the next 'crippler'! **20-24 points.** Twitcher. A good try. You should be well on your way to a big list. **15-19 points.** Birder. You are not really trying hard enough. Think of the tick, not of other people. **10-14 points.** Birdwatcher. Your heart is not really in it. Stick to local tetrad surveys. **Less than 10 points.** Dude. You appear to be a stupid, aggressive, masochistic defeatist, but you've probably got friends.

AUTHOR'S ACKNOWLEDGEMENTS

A great many people have contributed to this book (some of them unintentionally) and my thanks go to all of them. My special thanks go to: Jonathan Osborne, who helped with story material; John Haw, who helped compile the questions; Bill and Ruby at the "*Coot and Corncrake*", who provided much liquid inspiration; and all the regulars who helped and encouraged me, in particular Del, Ali and Chris. I would also like to thank Ted and Jackie for providing a peaceful haven and a word processor, Crispin Fisher for his help and encouragement and for his delightful artwork. I owe a great debt of gratitude to Robert Gillmor for allowing us to use the artwork from his excellent B.T.O annual dinner menus; to Paul Cemmick for so vividly illustrating the goings-on of Twitchett and his friends; and to Norman Arlott and the noble house of Collins for allowing us to use extracts from their more unorthodox correspondence. Finally, my thanks to Robert MacDonald, begetter of this book, for his inspiration and patience.

ILLUSTRATIONS

Norman Arlott. Page 67. Paul Cemmick. Pages 8, 11, 23, 31, 49, 63, 80, 90. Crispin Fisher. 16, 17, 28, 29, 42, 43, 56, 57, 64/65, 96, 97. Robert Gillmor. 46, 55, 79, 87, 95, 100, 115.